Can You ~~Should~~ Write A Book !

How to Write What You Know and Self-Publish Your Way to Success

BARBARA BINGHAM AND JEFFREY R. ORENSTEIN, PHD

You Can Write A Book:

How to Write What You Know and Self-Publish Your Way to Success

© Suncoast Digital Press, 2014

ISBN: 978-1-939237-14-9

Dedications

This work is dedicated to Virginia Orenstein, for her incredible support, encouragement and assistance in all my writing and business endeavors.

Jeff Orenstein

This book is dedicated to Trudy Radford, for her unwavering encouragement of me, and so many others.

Barbara Bingham

Contents

Introduction 1

This Book Is For You If…..1

Why This Self-Publishing Book Is Different 2

How To Leverage New Technology: Authority Marketing 5

If The Message Is Important, The Medium Is Important 5

How To Tune In To Your Own Inner Author 7

There Is No Reason To Hold Back....................................9

What To Do With Your Book Or Ebook Once It Is Done 9

How To Use This Book 10

Chapter I
Your Inner Author 11

Your Connection to the World 11

Awaken The Author Within You 12

There Are Recognized Experts In Every Field…Why Not You? 13

Is The Very Definition Of "Reading" Changing? 14

Who Has Time To Build Relationships When The Business Is Bustling Or Burning?...15

Have EBooks Made Printed Books Completely Obsolete?............................16

"But I'm A Lawyer, Not A Writer." 18

Key Distinctions For This Chapter 20

Summary..21

Chapter II
Defining Your Aim, Targeting and Hitting Your Topic 23

From Here to There: Which Road Connects You With Your Readers?..........24

Why Write A Book? 25

Who Needs You? 28

How Will The Reader Use Your Book?...........................28

Ask Yourself "What Can I Do To Set Myself Apart?" 29

Three Converging Circles Are Your Keys to Unlock A Hit Topic for Your Book...30

How To Choose Your Ideal Book Topic..........................31

Why Two Out Of Three Is Never Good Enough...32

Key Distinctions For This Chapter 35

Summary..36

Chapter III
What Is The Right Length For Your EBook? 37

Pages And Dynamic Elements Matter..37

Understanding Length Choice For The EBook Version Of Your Book 38

Factors Affecting eBook Length 41

EBook Types And Target Lengths 43

White Paper EBook 43

Short EBook...44

Medium EBook (Typical)..45

Long EBook...45

Knowing When To Say "Good — Enough!" A Checklist: 47

Key Distinctions For This Chapter 49

Summary..50

Chapter IV
Book Titles...51

How To Write Powerful, Magnetic Titles And Subtitles 51

Stand Out Among Thousands Of Competitors: A Title Is Your Billboard 52

Subtitles: Can A Book Live Without One? 53

What Problem Are You Going To Solve?..54

How Are You Going To Get Their Attention?..55

Great Title vs. Good Title 56

108 Power Verbs For Making a Good Title (or Subtitle) Great 56

Key Words 57

How Long Is A Great Title? 58

Key Words + Magnetic Charge = Powerfully Attractive, Great Title............59

Pinpoint Your Person Of Interest (Your Target Reader).................................61

Find and Push Your Target Reader's Hot Button..61

There Are No Digital Stone Tablets – A Title Can Be Changed More Easily
Than You Think...62

Key Distinctions for this Chapter 63

Summary...64

Chapter V
Beginning The Writing Process 65

Steps To Advance Toward Your Goals...65

Listen To, And Trust Yourself:
You Have All You Need To Write A Book 66

The Idea Collection Process 66

Categorizing Ideas 68

The Mind Map: Building The Bridge From Brainstorm To Book 69

Challenging Your Brain With Mind-Mapping 69

Giving Form to Your Thoughts 71

A Brief Catalogue of Proven Format Models..................................72

Nonfiction Book Format Examples 72

The # Of Ways to Do Something Book, or the How To __ Book..................72

The Avoiding Mistakes Book 72

Ask The Guru Book 73

Collection Of Others' Wisdom Or Stories.......................................73

Memoirs Or Biography..73

Timeless Words Book...74

The Season Premiere Book...75

You've Named The 'Who' And Developed The 'What' … Now For
The 'How'..76

Key Distinctions For This Chapter 76

Summary...77

Chapter VI
An Outline For Book/EBook Success 79

Every Book Needs A Great Outline —Here's How To Create Yours 79

An Outline For Book and eBook Success 80

Advantages Of An Outline 81

Defining The Book Outline 81

Outline Techniques..82

How To Write Your Outline...83

Use Tools You Know 83

Choose A Style 84

Formal? Casual? Use An Outline Style That Fits You 84

The Book/Ebook Express:
A Three-Step Method From Outline To Finish Line 85

Example: Author Outline Produced With The Ebook Express Method.........85

Writing Your Book From Your Outline 87

Key Distinctions For This Chapter 88

Summary 88

Chapter VII
Assemble Your Resources 89

Tools, Technology And Your Checklist For Self-Publishing Success 89

Assemble Your Writing and Technology Resources 90

Checklist of Writing Resources For True Self-Publishers 90

Non Computer technology 91

Computer Technology 95

Key Distinction For This Chapter...97

Summary 98

Chapter VIII
Cover Design 99

Capture Your Audience With A Great Book Cover.........................99

A Cover Can Crush Your Success Or Send You Soaring 100

You *Will* Be Judged By Your Cover So Take Advantage Of It 100

Choosing Your Ideal Cover Elements:
What Is Your Category Or Book Type? 101

Can You Read And Understand The Title's Words In Less Than
Three Seconds? 102

What Colors Communicate Your Brand And Appeal To Your Ideal
Target Reader? 103

Should You Use A Full Spectrum Of Colors Or A High Contrast
Two-Color Cover? 103

Can Your Cover Stand On Its Own? 104

Yes! You Need A BACK Cover For Your eBook 106

What Goes On A Back Cover? 107

It Never Hurts To Ask 110

Bullet Point Your Key Benefits for Readers 112

Bring The Reader To Your Web Site 112

Other Elements For The Back Cover...113

How Important Is The Cover To Your Book's Marketing Plan? 113

Book Covers: When to Hold Them, When to Fold Them...........................116

Key Distinctions For This Chapter 117

Summary..118

Chapter IX
The Dynamic eBook...119

Making Your Manuscript Sing and Dance..119

What Is A Dynamic Ebook? 120

Enhanced Ebooks Give Authors More Power To Reach Readers................121

What Makes A Book "Dynamic"? 122

Practical Dynamic eBook Elements 124

Don't Forget Traditional eBook Elements 126

Using Dynamic eBook Elements Effectively 127

Creating Dynamic eBook Elements:
Technology Harnessed In Service Of Ideas..128

Creating Your Dynamic Elements Step By Step 130

Creating Dynamic eBook Photographs 130

Creating Dynamic eBook Video..131

Creating Dynamic eBook Audio 135

Creating Dynamic eBook Animations...136

Creating Dynamic eBook Hyperlinks..137

Key Distinctions For This Chapter 139

Summary..140

Chapter X
Transforming A Manuscript Into An EBook.........................141

Using Technology To Reach Your Target Readers 141

Digital Publishing: The Technical Environment 142

Key Considerations For Selecting The Right Publishing Tools 143

The All-Important Publishing Tool 144

Targeting Your eBook Display Device 145

Document Format And File Storing Decisions Are Important......................147

Do I Need to Use the ISBN System?...148

Copyright and Copyright Registration:
Protecting Your Intellectual Property 150

POD: What about Print-On-Demand Services? 151

Keep Your Eye On The Goal...152

Key Distinctions For This Chapter 153

Summary...154

Chapter XI
Marketing: The Book/EBook Success Secret 155

The Author's Reward: Achieving Readership..156

Five Book Marketing Actions To Take *Before* Your Book Is Published......157

Sales And Marketing Scaled For The Self-Publisher 159

Become Irresistibly Attractive To Your Target Audience 160

Just Try One Bite… 161

Find Your Audience And Turn The Spotlight On 162

"You Are Cordially Invited …To My List" 163

Where Preparation Meets Opportunity: Finding Luck In List-Building 164

First-Name Basis 165

Community And Extended Contacts 165

The World (Wide Web) Is Your Oyster! 166

Creating Your eBook Marketing Plan: A Critical Step 167

Your Book Marketing Plan...168

Action Step: Begin Your Marketing Plan..168

Suncoast Digital Press Marketing Plan Outline...169

Smart Authors Engage In Pre-Publication Marketing 172

Identify Your Target Reader...172

Be One *In* A Million…. Not One *Of* A Million 173

Broadcast Your Book's *Benefits* For Your Target Reader
On *Their* Radio Station 174

Optimize Your Title..174

Target Reader Locales 175

Distribution And Where To Publish 177

Creating Smart (Win-Win) Alliances 177

Introducing Your Book to the World..179

PR: Make a Splash Without Much Cash 179

Promotion and Publicity 180

Who Cares? Identify Your Best Broadcasters 180

Your Internet Presence 185

Blogs..186

Article Marketing..187

Speeches 187

Regional Author Tours 189

Virtual Author Tours 190

Email..191

Book Video Trailer 191

Targeted Display or Web Advertising..192

Keep The Marketing Engine Stoked:
It Takes Time To Build An Empire 193

It's Okay To Admit You Have Your Next Book Already In Mind.............195

Key Distinctions For This Chapter 198

Summary..198

Suncoast Digital Press Self-Publishing Marketing Cheat Sheet....................199

Chapter XII
Tracking Success..201

Readers, Sales and Revenue & Measuring Market Response........................201

Tracking Success 202

What Is Book Tracking?..202

Why Track? 203

What To Track 205

How To Track 207

Sustaining Your Tracking...211

Key Distinctions For This Chapter 212

Summary..212

Chapter XIII
Get Set To Soar And Sustain Your Success 213

Cleared for Takeoff...214

Don't Rush To Take Off Into The Publishing World:
Get Ahead Of Potential Mistakes With A Thorough Pre-Flight Check 214

Editing And Proofreading: The Author's Best Friends 215

Proofreading Checklist 216

The Need for Speed: Book Readers Appreciate an Index 217

Formats Are Fickle: Converting For Publication Requires Mastery 218

Don't Take Off Without A Flight Plan...219

Know Your Indicators and Check Your Instruments To Measure Them......222

Take-Off Is Not The End Goal – It's The Beginning....................................223

Flying The Friendly Skies: Your Plan For Continued Success 224

You Are Ready for Take-Off. Push the Throttle NOW...............................225

Key Distinction For This Chapter..225

Summary...225

Epilogue **227**

Acknowledgements **229**

Contact The Authors **231**

About The Authors **235**

Introduction

This Book Is For You If...

Welcome to the world of nonfiction book (and especially eBook) writing. By picking up this book you have already demonstrated an interest in riding the crest of the first great marketing wave of the 21st century, the self-publishing revolution. If you are a professional, entrepreneur, author – or anyone who wants to control his or her own destiny – you will find this book's steps, process details, and encouraging style to be immediately useful, practical and valuable. This book is for the goal-minded person ready to act and accomplish writing and publishing a book, so the content is high-value how-to information, not just interesting ideas *about* writing and self-publishing; you have here material to *use*, not just read. Perhaps best of all, you will find that there is no actual mystery in the process of book writing despite the mystique that surrounds published authors.

You are invited to watch this two-minute video introduction by one of our authors, Barbara Bingham. (In the eBook version of this book, this is one of the dynamic elements. In this print version, we have embedded this QR code for your convenience.) If you don't want to view this using a smartphone free App, the next time you go to YouTube, look up the Suncoast Digital Press channel where you will find this clip and several short videos which are *directly* related to this book.

Even if you've never written any book before, this book will guide, teach, coach and empower you to write and publish your book. It is intended for those who are willing to invest in themselves, see their book project all the way through, and follow our steps for putting it to work tirelessly for you 24/7 to build your personal brand, create a passive income stream, and/or leave a legacy.

Professionals who have used our steps and processes report that, as published authors, they have more professional self-confidence and the enhanced credibility they garner helps to build trusting relationships with their clients and prospective clients. The new *selling* is now *connecting*. Writing a book will help you connect, perhaps better than any other strategy, with your target market. As you follow our guidance, you will not just write *any* book in order to create an information product and become an "infopreneur" – you will learn how to utilize state-of-the art technology to deliver an impressive and valuable package of your best ideas, and become a recognized authority in your field.

Who has the time or budget these days for expensive display or broadcast advertising, awkward elevator speeches, or short-lived tri-fold brochures? With your own published book, you will have a highly effective tool to attract the kind of attention you want from the media, the marketplace and your peers. You will have a tangible and magnetic product to use in attracting people in your chosen target audience to your web site, to your speaking engagements and to your business.

In addition to leveraging your book to help your business, if you so choose (and you do retain all the decision-making power when you bypass the outdated methods of traditional publishing houses) you will learn how to make your own Agreements with Barnes & Noble, Amazon and other top on-line booksellers. The Internet allows you to easily promote and sell your book in order to provide you with a passive income stream and get your message out to the world, and you'll find out how to do that right here in this book.

Why This Self-Publishing Book Is Different

You could stock an incredible bookstore just from the books written by some of the authors who have chosen to self-publish their books. You probably recognize a few of these famous self-publishers: Margaret Atwood, William Blake, Ken Blanchard,

Robert Bly, Lord Byron, Willa Cather, Pat Conroy, Alexander Dumas, T.S. Eliot, Benjamin Franklin, Zane Grey, Nathaniel Hawthorne, Ernest Hemingway, Stephen King, Rudyard Kipling, Louis L'Amour, D.H. Lawrence, Rod McKuen, John Muir, Anais Nin, Thomas Paine, Tom Peters, Edgar Allen Poe, Alexander Pope, Beatrix Potter, Ezra Pound, Marcel Proust, Carl Sandburg, Robert Service, George Bernard Shaw, Upton Sinclair, Gertrude Stein, William Strunk, Alfred Lord Tennyson, Henry David Thoreau, Leo Tolstoi, Mark Twain, Walt Whitman and Virginia Woolf.

There are many other amazing authors who have chosen to self-publish at some time in their careers. You would do well to be among this honored group.

Ben Franklin, using the pen name of Richard Saunders, self-published his *Poor Richard's Almanack* in 1732 and continued to produce the almanac for another 26 years. Many of his famous sayings came from the *Almanack*. Because of the success of his writing and publishing business, Franklin was able to retire at the age of 42 and focus on becoming one of the world's greatest scientists and inventors, culminating his life as a statesman and one of the key founders of the United States of America as a signer of the Declaration of Independence.

While a lot has changed in the writing and publishing world since Ben Franklin's time, this is not simply a book of updated theory – it's a practical handbook of state-of-the-art specifics. We've used ourselves and our own books as guinea pigs, refining our craft and sharpening our expertise. We are able to let you know what works and what doesn't. It is not only our synthesized story, but the story of many of our clients and professionals just like you. It is the distillation of many decades of collective experience in the fields of writing, publishing, business coaching, teaching and marketing.

As the Pew Research Center study published in a landmark April 2012 report, "The rise of eBooks in American Culture is part of a larger story about a shift from printed to digital material." As part of this wave, more and more professionals, entrepreneurs, executives, professional speakers, coaches, consultants and others who communicate their expertise as an integral part of their business are realizing that the discipline needed for writing, publishing and marketing a book is a great way to organize their own thoughts on a subject. It is also a superb vehicle for demonstrating their expertise and authority in their chosen field, and for becoming a go-to expert for present and future clients.

What Pew reported as "The rise of eBooks in American culture" has put successful self-publishing within the reach of far more people than ever before and simultaneously made it both practical and respectable. The publishing and book marketing paradigms have shifted and they are not going to shift back. There has never been a better time to be an author. It has never been easier to reach those who can benefit from your ideas.

When best-selling authors are cutting out the "middlemen" (large traditional publishing houses or seldom-reliable book agents) and going directly to their readers via independent publishing, it is safe to say that the day has passed when self-publishing was equated with the infamy of paying a "subsidy publisher" or "vanity press." Today, self-publishing has come of age. One reason why more than 75% of the books published in the US today are self-published is that the author gets to keep significantly more money from each book sold. Besides skipping the huge percentage traditional publishers keep, an independent author has the right to sell his/her book for any price, and in fact can sell it through their own web site or channels which allow them to keep 100% of the revenue.

Self-publishing is an exciting alternative to the millions of rejection slips unpublished authors collect each year. Repeated rejection can ruin the hopes and dreams of even highly qualified authors. For the person who wants to write a quality book with the help of a professional editor, choose their own publishing package and marketing plan, and complete their project in less than half the time of those outdated publishing houses, we have great news! There is finally a readily available and affordable opportunity and this book will show you exactly how to capitalize on it.

How To Leverage New Technology: Authority Marketing

Through the past several thousand years, the *book* has become the ultimate symbol of authority. You have a *book* inside you. You know how to do something better than anyone else in the world. If you doubt that, just remember that there is no one better at being *you*, and *you* are uniquely experienced and uniquely qualified to share your experience-based knowledge, lessons, perspectives and wisdom.

If you are a professional in private practice or an entrepreneur, you feel you have a product or an idea or a vision that stands out among your competitors. How do you let the world know about your unique qualifications? A business card won't cut it. Even if people don't throw it away, it does not do justice to your specialness, your distinct brand which should stand out in a crowd. And everyone's got a website with an "About" button.

What works today, superbly, is to put your ideas in a book. Consider this example: You're a brand new home health care company. Your research tells you there are a significant number of people out there in the position of needing to learn about and hire a home health care provider. Often that person is caught unprepared and suddenly needs answers and guidance. You have the expert answers they are desperate to know. You have high-value information. Write it down. People will seek you out before contacting others who many offer practically the same service or product, but lack your status as the person "who wrote the book" on the subject.

If The Message Is Important, The Medium Is Important

In this book you will learn how to present what you know – the latest thinking, proven principles and examples from your own real-life experiences – in a clear, interesting and accessible fashion. Don't make the mistake of imagining that your knowledge of the topic of interest to your niche market is already dispersed and widely available. You are the owner of substantial intellectual property which could be organized into a unique book and viewed as a valuable asset by others who want or need a fast way to know what you have learned.

But you may be thinking, "Am I really an *authority*? Sure, I can do the self-promotion and social marketing to position myself as a guru, but am I just using technology to fool people?"

We can help you to resolve this issue. When you present yourself as a professional with something valuable to say, and your medium is a high-quality, well-written book, you have the opportunity to connect in a profound way. This book is written to help you choose the ideal topic, start and finish a book, and have it published. Your book will become not only a reputation-builder but also a tangible information product you can sell via the Internet and social media to a large target audience, or give away as one of the *Attraction Marketing* strategies you will learn later in the chapter on marketing.

While there are many actions you can take to help establish yourself as an expert, writing one or more books is considered a necessary step toward attaining "authority" status. In an article in CIO magazine about the top ten gurus in Information Technology, every one of the IT professionals had written at least one book. Remember, historically and today, a book symbolizes authority. It is a fact that one press release announcing your book can impart "instant credibility" in the view of media contacts, professional peers and your target readers.

Authoring a book also gives experts and entrepreneurs fresh visibility and credibility – a reason to be news. Book authors have "most-favored" status with media producers, meeting planners, and keynote speaker booking agents. Whether it's through a press release to the media, an update on your social media profile, an announcement in your company newsletter or blog, or an email to friends and family, you will have some exciting news to share! And having a book gives you an unequaled promotional piece – brochures are tossed while books are saved and often shared. (Digital libraries are growing rapidly as eBooks are even more easily saved, stored, and shared than printed books.) The only potential downside to becoming a published author is that, indeed, you will become more well-known. Therefore, paying close attention to developing a well-written, professionally-edited book, as we will show you exactly how to do, is critical.

You want to enhance your credibility, not destroy it with a thrown-together, amateurish attempt – there are enough of those on Amazon already! By following this book and investing a little more effort than most other people, you will end up with a book you are proud of and which has strong appeal to others. You will be more known, and more respected than ever before.

How To Tune In To Your Own Inner Author

This book is essential for business owners, attorneys, doctors, ministers, educators, speakers, professional coaches, therapists, thought leaders – anyone who wants to share their expertise and capitalize on their experience by attracting new clients, or new personal or business community members in the process.

Others who find this book useful are retirees who want to share their life experience and wisdom as a way to both be actively engaged in a rewarding project and also build their legacy. In thirteen chapters, we walk you through everything you may need to employ to start, finish, and publish your book. We assume you have a good command of English, can dedicate time to focus on your book, and are in touch with personal goals for your book which genuinely excite you. For many people, the compelling reason for writing a book has nothing to do with book royalties…they have simply gotten to the point where it is harder to keep their message inside than to share it with others. It is true that for nearly every author, the personal satisfaction achieved by writing, completing and publishing a book dwarfs all the business and financial rewards.

The hard part, as in swimming, is to take the plunge. The water looks so cold! Can it be warmed up? Yes, we've taken care of that and you can now accept the invitation to jump in. Not only are you going to get off to a good start, you will be able to use this book as your guide at each step of the way.

After just one chapter, Chapter I: *Your Inner Author: Your Connection to the World,* you will wonder why you waited so long to write your book. You will start to see exactly what you already have at hand, and what you need to gather to get started.

In Chapter II: *Defining Your Aim, Target and Hit Topic*, you will begin to have a perfectly sharp image of your target reader. People may write a book for any number of good personal reasons – fame, income, therapy, recollection and/or validation of their lives. But what they produce will have a validity of its own to the extent that it's useful to somebody else. You will learn that books that are too general (a book on fishing, for example) may be interesting to read but will not help anyone to learn how to (actually) do something, such as catching a spottail bass. To discuss one's enjoyment of fishing may feed another's imagination for the moment, but to clearly write about the intricacies of fishing, the best equipment, locations and techniques (of course with many fishing tales included) allows the reader to feed his appetite for both sport and sustenance.

The crucial thing to remember, as you jump in, is that it's true that any number of books have already been written on a given topic – but not *your* book. *You* are going to personally select the aspect of the broad topic which you know well and want to write about, and you are going to share your unique take on that aspect. There are two essential elements of a nonfiction book: subject and theme. The *subject* is what your book is about: the issue, event or person it deals with. The *theme* is what you want to say about the subject – what you bring to the subject from your experience, perspective or new ideas on the topic.

As in the example of writing a book about fishing, if you're an experienced angler you have plenty of original material and you own the intellectual property rights to all of it. *Your* knowledge and perspective and unique problem-solving experiences while, say, fishing for spottail bass in Florida, *are* book-worthy. But where do you start?

Think back to a time when you *did not know* what you now *know* about your subject. How did you get to *here* from *there*? What steps did you take, what mistakes did you make, and what lessons did you learn? What chance events helped you, or was it a mentor? Of all the many things you've learned since the time when you were clueless but curious, which are most important? You can't tell your reader *everything* you've done, but what are the absolute gems they almost certainly don't know but could really benefit from knowing?

There Is No Reason To Hold Back

Writing is not always easy. But it is both satisfying and practical. As John Grisham wrote, "Writing's still the most difficult job I've ever had - but it's worth it."

Don't have time to write it? You can dictate it or have a ghostwriter do it for you. And you don't need 75,000 words, you can do it in 20,000 words. If you want to write less and still tell more, add some photos and dynamic elements such as video or audio. Are you unsure if your writing is polished enough for the public? Your editor will make you look good. Any other nagging concerns stopping you from starting? Make this book your constant companion and we'll walk with you through the whole journey. You know what to tell yourself: "Just do it!" Or as another inspiring quotation tells us, "Boldness has genius, power, and magic in it!"

What To Do With Your Book Or Ebook Once It Is Done

Publishing a book and/or eBook and marketing it to your chosen reader so it does not languish in digital anonymity are not easy, which is good for you because not just anyone can make it happen. Fortunately, good writing, the steps of independent publishing, and book marketing can be learned. This book provides practical techniques and tips to learn the craft of book writing, to understand the evolving world of self-publishing and marketing, and to empower you to put what you learn to work for both personal satisfaction and professional advancement. Chapter XI: *Marketing: The Book/eBook Success Secret* is power-packed with everything useful about today's marketing strategies – hundreds of specific tips and tools it would take years for an individual to assemble.

How To Use This Book

As a tool designed to teach nonfiction, business-oriented writing and self-publishing, this book is organized into self-paced chapters. Such a format constitutes a practical way to learn the craft of nonfiction writing and independent publishing and fit the project work into your busy life.

The body of each chapter is written to explain, to answer questions, and to make some recommendations about techniques that work. We have stayed away from jargon and stuck to the workable, proven and practical. At the end of each chapter, you will find a summary of key points and key distinctions.

Because we know that people have different learning styles, levels of interest, and spare time, we have put a lot of emphasis on self-paced learning. As the renowned 18th century philosopher and prolific author Jean Jacques Rousseau observed, "However great a man's natural talent may be, the act of writing cannot be learned all at once."

If you are like many very busy and successful professionals, you know that you should have a book for professional advancement, but also know that you have very little time to write it. This book will still come in handy for you because it provides you with a comprehensive tool for everything involved in writing, publishing and marketing a book or eBook, all in one place. For the person who would rather not invest the total time themselves, this book provides the necessary background to understand the process when you retain somebody to write your book for you, and to manage the project to a successful conclusion.

It is time to begin your journey to becoming a published author. Your whole life has prepared you for it. Let's get started.

Chapter 1

Your Inner Author

Your Connection to the World

Awaken The Author Within You

For how many years have you had thoughts to write and publish a book? Do you have compelling, personal goals in mind which you can achieve by becoming a published author? Do you want the fame and increased business that comes from being published and becoming an in-demand authority in your field?

Yes, there is very probably an author residing within you. If so, you are in good company. A widely quoted survey by the Jenkins Group, Inc., a Michigan publishing services firm, found that 81 percent of Americans feel they should write a book.

Quite a few Americans have actually realized their publishing dream. The United Nations Educational, Scientific and Cultural Organization (UNESCO) in 2011 reported that there were 288,355 new titles and editions published in the USA.

A recent survey we conducted showed that most people believe that *everyone* has a book in them. Is your book ready to come out? You are the sum of your experiences, relationships and education. You may need to simply shift your thinking from wondering if you are capable of being "an author" or if you could dare call yourself "a writer" to simply asking yourself "What would I like to say, and to whom?" Some of you already have written articles, blogs, journals, speeches or training material, or you have good ideas and dreams of writing and would love to see yourself one day proudly holding a published book with your name on the cover.

If you are reading this, the chances are good that you are one of the vast majority of Americans who has the true author's passion but is not yet published. Perhaps you have had others tell you that "you should write a book!" And you've told yourself that, yet put it off. This book is going to help you change that – you absolutely can write, finish and publish your book. Also, if you are a professional or entrepreneur, you are always on the lookout for a great new marketing tool. A self-published book or eBook accomplishes both goals, and can be completed in less time than you may imagine

You will notice this book thoroughly covers more about eBooks than most self-publishing books. Why the focus on eBooks vs. traditionally printed books? Although publishing your book as an eBook avoids the major cost of production, printing, inventory and distribution, it is by no means the only reason to create a digital (electronic) version even if you want or need some quantity of traditionally printed and bound books. The fact is, more and more people are choosing to read books on screens instead of paper. Recent statistics show:

- EBook sales have jumped from 323 million in 2008 to 9 billion in 2013.

- E-reader sales in 2013 are expected to top 14 million.

- Barnes & Noble will generate 1 billion dollars in revenue in 2013 from digital books.

EBooks have surpassed printed books and audio book sales on Amazon, the largest bookseller on the Internet. E-Readers like Kindle and Nook are selling by the millions. The Amazon eBook store has, to date, four authors who have each sold more than one million eBooks.

There Are Recognized Experts In Every Field…Why Not You?

Becoming an author has always been a way to make a statement about yourself, your knowledge, and your confidence in your own ideas. It's up to you to position yourself as an expert, or as someone with something worthwhile to say. Publishing a book is the fast track to arriving at authority status and can open many doors of opportunity. Your book will:

- Build relationships and connect you with your tribe (target audience.)

- Be the foundation product to build into multiple profit-building products.

- Consistently bring in more and higher-paying speaking and consulting opportunities.

- Win the attention of publishers and distributors or book reviewers.

For example, a licensed marriage and family counselor reports that she is convinced that being able to say she is a "published author" has helped her professional reputation more than if she had gone back to school for a Ph.D. Her book provided the extra credibility she sought to advance her business. A corporate event planner shared that when she is booking a keynote speaker, she expects the speaker to have a book they have authored to offer at the back of the meeting room. If she were evaluating two possible speakers to hire, the one with the book would win out. They have more credibility, she explains.

Is The Very Definition Of "Reading" Changing?

Notice how the above list sounds more like a marketing strategy than an exercise in writing? Your book and/or eBook will replace obsolete advertising and promotional efforts and will give you a powerful advantage to reach your market. Now more than ever you must engage your prospective and existing clients by standing out, giving value, and developing relationships. People want to feel related, interacted with, *connected*. People "follow" people they are interested in via social media such as "twitter." One-way communication has given way to two-way communication. For example, instead of simply listening to a news commentator on television, or a musical artist's song on the radio, a person can go to a Facebook page, or send them an email, or tweet with them on Twitter – all of which create a sense of interaction and relationship, whether it is real or only perceived.

People, many of them business people, start a conversation with strangers via a blog post and receive comments and carry on conversations across the globe. "Reading" someone's blog can mean you actually converse back and forth through your keyboard, or it could mean you watch their YouTube video posts and have a virtual experience of them or what they are teaching. Seth Godin, best-selling author and marketing genius, talks about this sea change of how people now sort themselves into groups who share an attraction for a particular message, largely through the advent of social media. In his book *Tribes,* Godin urges entrepreneurs to become leaders of a tribe (also called a niche market, target market or target audience.)

Who Has Time To Build Relationships When The Business Is Bustling Or Burning?

Are you satisfied with how much time you spend each week working *on* your business as compared to *in* your business? Most business owners are too challenged to step out of the daily demands and focus on strategic planning and marketing, even when they know they are responsible for that role. With their time at a premium, a professional in private practice or an entrepreneur must utilize the most effective (and affordable) tools available.

Now is the opportune time to create a state-of-the-art marketing tool: a book, and ideally, an enhanced, dynamic eBook which will work tirelessly for you 24/7 once you set it in motion via the Internet. Enhanced eBooks which include embedded multimedia components such as video and audio are what are called "dynamic" eBooks.

The eBook revolution has created a practical and effective publishing medium that is well-suited to modern authors in general, and especially to business authors because it excels at presenting information in ways today's market demands. When you succeed in genuinely engaging your target reader (a task made easier with dynamic elements) it follows that your reader will feel more connected with you, and your relationship can build from there.

Have EBooks Made Printed Books Completely Obsolete?

Many potential authors (and quite a few experienced and well-published authors) are confused about how to define an eBook. Is it a certain size? Do you have to own a Kindle or a Nook to read one? Do you download it onto your computer and then print it out with your printer? Is it just like a book or manuscript but it's read on an electronic device?

First, a book is still a book, even in the digital age. The final form a book takes can be ink on printed pages bound into what we traditionally call a book, but today books can also be in the form of a computer-generated file that is readable on a desktop or laptop computer, tablet, e-reader or even a smart phone – or all of them. That is what we know as an "eBook." (The "e" simply stands for electronic, like the "e" in email.)

The eBook revolution has made self-publishing (with and without professional assistance) so popular and accepted that even famous best-selling authors who previously went with big New York publishing houses are abandoning their former publishers. They enjoy the freedom and cost-savings, plus have much more control over their work. Authors as renowned as J.K. Rowling and Stephen King are traveling the self-publishing road and building relationships directly with their readers. More and more famous and not-yet-famous authors are leaving the expense and quick obsolescence of traditional bound and printed books behind and helping to invent the future of publishing. EBooks have already changed the publishing world forever.

Do we recommend an author publish printed, bound books? Yes. In conjunction with publishing your eBook you can have any number of printed copies, and thanks to new Print-On-Demand (POD) technology, you no longer have to order and inventory hundreds or thousands of books to have each printed book be very affordable. These soft-cover, printed books are useful for many promotional purposes including to sell at seminars or trade shows where you meet your readers in person and they can walk away with your (autographed) book. Even if the original plan is to write an eBook, once the manuscript is complete most people think it makes sense to have both versions and in some cases an audio version.

Ben, a professional speaker, always has a stack of his printed book in the back of the room for his audience to purchase after his presentation. He believes the crowd is warmed up and eager to purchase his book then, but may not be as motivated later if he only had an eBook version and they had to go later to his web site or the Amazon Kindle store to download it electronically. It's a little more trouble for him to carry and sell physical books, but he charges a premium. One reason he says he can do this is that his sales pitch is that you aren't just buying one book – you get two for the price of one, plus a bonus! This is accomplished by printing inside the physical book the download instructions and special code which allows purchasers of the print book to get the eBook at no additional charge.

Once at Ben's web site, in order to obtain the eBook version, the customer enters their contact information and then Ben can stay in touch with those customers in the future. Prior to this strategy, Ben usually had no way of knowing who attended his speech or who bought his book in the back of the room. Ben has two other books and, not surprisingly, the customers who come to the web site to get their free eBook see the video trailers for Ben's other books and often decide to purchase those as well. Again, Ben offers both print and electronic versions of all his books because he has discovered that, at least in his target market, the two versions sell equally well.

At this time we would agree that most authors should consider offering both versions, and in a later chapter, we will show you a simple way to accomplish that. It is called Print-On-Demand and uses slightly modified files similar to the ones which you need for producing an eBook. Only a few years ago an author who was not being published by a big publishing house would have to order hundreds or thousands of books from a "vanity press."

It is not an overnight process but if you follow the right route to publishing success, you will arrive at the wonderful day that your book is published sooner than you ever imagined. We know that writing a high-quality book is a big task, but we're here to give you the guidance and technology that you need to start and finish your book and join the elite club of successful professional and business authors.

This self-paced book is the only handbook you need to actually get those great book ideas out of your head and down on paper (or its electronic equivalent) and then to get your book published and in front of those who can benefit from your ideas. It's easy to give readers the choice of printed or electronic versions, but remember that first you have to write the book!

"But I'm A Lawyer, Not A Writer."

As writers and editors who have dealt with many business and professional writers, we know there is an author in almost every professional or entrepreneur, even those who have convinced themselves that writing is something to be feared rather than embraced. Together, we can not only help you find your voice as an author, we can work with you to make your message clear and your book a success.

If you have written articles for industry publications or to offer on your web site, you have a good start to either creating a book which includes your previous writing, or developing a book one chapter at a time just as if you were writing a series of articles. You are about to learn how to start, outline, finish, title, publish and market your book. Following our steps, you can do it all yourself, or you can learn how to choose the right editors and publishing partners when you need help or want to accelerate the completion of your book project.

We are strong advocates of the eBook revolution and encourage and teach authors how to capitalize on the many benefits of digital publishing. More than just an electronic version of a book, we think that to catch the wave of successful publishing you should produce a book which, at least to some degree, is state-of-the-art and enhanced with elements which today's technology allows. More and more, eBook readers are expecting a multimedia experience, not just words on a page. This book will help you understand which elements are best suited for your particular book and show you how to incorporate them. To produce a great eBook you have to master the several non-compatible major iterations of dynamic digital technology or delegate this to those with experience.

Note that while embedding dynamic (multimedia) elements does not add much cost to the eBook formatting process, author royalty revenues may be reduced if booksellers such as Amazon charge a fee to the author (not the customer) each time the dynamic eBook is downloaded. This is because that download uses the bookseller's bandwidth, which means the more multimedia content in the book, the higher the charges that may be incurred. A simple way to avoid this is to upload your video, for example, to YouTube or Vimeo and/or to your own web site and put a hyperlink in your eBook. (The downside to this is that the reader has to be connected to the Internet for the link to work.) Take advantage of the fact this eBook is enhanced with several video links and click on them, as you were invited to do at the beginning of our *Introduction*.

Key Distinctions For This Chapter

Connecting vs. Prospecting   Advertising your products and services to get in front of your target prospects is no longer enough for successful marketing. You must also motivate people to join you in communications which will build connection and trust. An excellent and proven enticement is a targeted, content-rich book or eBook, and the best vehicle to get your message out there is the Internet and social media duo.

EBook Publishing vs. Traditional Print Publishing   An electronic version of a book (an eBook) is created, published and transmitted via digital processors (computers, etc.) One main differentiating advantage this provides is that distribution is significantly faster and cheaper. Rather than wait for a publisher to print and ship books, you can have a self-published eBook up for sale on Amazon, Barnes & Noble or other online bookstores the same day you finish proofing and formatting your manuscript. Also, an interested reader does not have to make a trip to the book store or wait for an ordered book to be shipped to them — they can download an eBook and be reading it within minutes of their decision. Be that as it may, printed books are still widely popular and should not be ignored as a second version to offer the readers who prefer that format.

Authority/Guru/Tribe Leader vs. Writer/Author   As a professional or entrepreneur, becoming a published author positions you as a recognized authority. Your expertise in your field is what's important in order to write a book, not your previous experience as a writer or published author. Your knowledge, published in an engaging way, builds connection with your target audience, your *tribe*. The reader values how your book makes a difference for them personally more than if it simply shows literary prowess.

Summary

By following this book, you can write, edit and publish a book and you can leverage it to significantly help you professionally. Your book, printed or electronic, serves many purposes but the main focus of this book is to teach you how to use it as part of a modern marketing plan. While we are not abandoning the traditionally printed book, but because of the convenience and new technology that can add video, audio and other enhanced elements to your manuscript, state-of-the-art eBooks have several significant advantages.

- They can "sing and dance." In other words, because they are digital files, they can incorporate hyperlinks, audio, video, interactive quizzes, rich illustrations, slide shows and other similar multimedia features when the subject matter and the context within the book call for it. Once that is accomplished, you can have these dynamic elements appear on a variety of digital-capable devices like computers, e-readers or smart phones. This makes them superb media for communicating and illustrating ideas.

- As evidenced by the explosion in sales of Kindles, Nooks and other eBook reading devices, the eBook has become the most popular and convenient choice for millions of readers. People read eBooks on desktop computers, laptops, e-readers, tablets and even smart phones. EBooks fit the modern technology most of us have and depend upon.

- Because an eBook does not have to be specially prepared and formatted for a printing press, the actual book production process takes hours instead of weeks or even months.

- Distribution is dramatically easier and far less expensive compared to printed books because eBooks are sent via electronic files to the reader. There is no need for printing, binding, warehousing, packing and shipping, fighting for precious book store shelf space or accommodating publisher returns of unsold books.

- You can put eBooks on your website, build them into any social media page, tweet about them, write about them in your blog, and use the infinite resources of the Internet to build relationships with your target niche and market your book to them.

- If you want a few printed and bound copies, the same files that are used to produce an eBook can be easily modified and uploaded to a "print on demand" (POD) service and a few copies can be printed as needed in a cost-effective way. No more do authors have to buy hundreds or even thousands of books to get published by a "vanity press."

Chapter II

Defining Your Aim, Targeting and Hitting Your Topic

From Here to There: Which Road Connects You With Your Readers?

> "Until one is committed there is hesitancy, the chance to draw back, always ineffectiveness....Whatever you can do, or dream you can, begin it. Boldness has genius, power, and magic in it."
>
> — W.H. Murray
>
> (Journal excerpt during his expedition over the Himalayas)

Because you have already arrived right here, you are actually in a good place and quite far along your road to becoming a published author. Like the clichéd ham and eggs distinction, you are no longer like the chicken who is only "involved" – you are more like the pig who is truly "committed." Okay, you're *not* really like the pig in a literal sense. However, you are indeed committed and moving toward your goal. If you keep it up, you will reach your goal of writing and publishing a book sooner than you realize.

Like most worthwhile things in life, writing and publishing a book is a journey. Your path along this journey will be much easier and faster with the help of this book. Just as you have come to rely on the GPS when you drive, think of this book as your GPS to direct and position you for success with your book.

At this juncture along your road to publishing, you either have a very good idea about your book topic, or you haven't quite gotten that far yet. Either way, you are making significant progress and the thrill of having a clear topic and title is just around the bend. In this chapter we will help you explore several avenues to end up with a book concept, or with more clarity about the one you have been considering. Once that milestone is passed and you clarify your book topic, type, and format, you will be able to accelerate toward your goal quickly.

Why Write A Book?

An important consideration to clarify and integrate into your thought process is your goal as an author. What do you want to write about, and why?

The best way to find your answer is to start with an honest and thorough self-inventory of your own training, experience, writing ability, time to devote to your project, and the other things that qualify you as an author on a given topic. One easy way to do this is to access the "Author Self-Assessment" tool we have created and put on our web site. If you spend a few minutes thinking about the answers as you complete the form, you will gain some knowledge and perspective about your readiness to write a book, and have a better idea about the gaps which you need to focus on filling to become fully prepared.

Many times clients will tell us they are clear on their book idea and have plenty of information to fill it, however they don't have the time to actually write their book. Or they simply would rather spend their time doing what they already do best, not going through the learning curve of becoming an author. Because of this, "ghostwriting" services are popular for help with some or all of the outlining, writing and formatting required to produce a professional-looking, quality book. A ghostwriter is someone who writes the book but credits you as author – it's done all the time and is an option for busy professionals and entrepreneurs who can't find time to write but still want a book because of all the advantages it provides. If you are considering retaining one, our advice is to make certain that the ghostwriter you retain understands your goals and how your profession and experience need to be translated into a book that will accomplish your goals. Also, make sure that your ghostwriter has writing experience in your genre, probably a business book. A great novel writer is not also likely to be a great self-help or business writer.

Whether you write all, some, or none of it yourself, you and your ideas are the *source* of your book. Unless you strictly want a ghostwriter to take the time to interview you at length and write your book in a way that is congruent with your goals, you must be self-motivated (and even excited!) throughout the writing process to write a really good book. You need enough motivation and enthusiasm to envision and design your book project, work on it regularly, and see it all the way through. Merely wishing you had a collection of life stories recorded is not enough motivation to get your book written and published. Having an idea for an eBook to sell on Amazon for a great passive income stream is not enough motivation either. Even picturing an ultra-professional-looking book next to your headshot to boost your reputation in your field is not enough motivation.

So what constitutes sufficient motivation? A good way to answer is to imagine when your book completed, published and in hand, what, in that picture, are you most eager to do with your book? Who are you most excited to share it with? What is your intended result? There are many valid reasons to write a book and each one requires you to tailor what you write to your purpose.

For example, are you writing an eBook to impress present and future clients? If so, you should demonstrate your professional expertise and experience and offer a lot of practical real-world examples and experience. Are you writing your book as a professional or entrepreneur who wants to be considered a credible authority on a topic? If so, you will probably want to quote several other recognizable experts who agree with your positions and include a foreword or afterword from one of these experts who gives you some professional weight by implication. If you can picture the reader you are writing for and are excited about accomplishing specific goals, chances are pretty good that you have found your motivation, or what is often called your muse. Find yours and listen to it.

Two approaches to consider when you decide to write a book:

- **Author's strategy** – your desire is to write, get published, and make money from the royalties of book sales. Your focus is on writing a great book which is likely to be widely popular and which will become a best-seller, at least in its category. You need to first do the math. Remember that many books, especially eBooks, are sold today for a few dollars and the author only gets a percentage (which varies and is set by each bookseller.) If you spend any time and money promoting your book (which is not really optional) your book sales will have to be quite extraordinary for you to have an income worth mentioning strictly from the sale of your book.

- **Marketer's strategy** – you write a book because you know it is by far the best way to become more well-known for what you want to be known for. Having a book is like jet fuel for every single marketing effort you already have in place, from SEO work on your web site to speaking engagements, social networking, or blogging. You intend to leverage the fact you are a published author in order to achieve your income goals as a business owner or professional. The almost instant credibility which having a book gives you will provide what months or years of other types of marketing strategies could provide.

When does the "author's strategy" make perfect sense? When you already have a large following because your name is widely recognized. If you are as famous as Dr. Laura or Tom Brokaw or Stephen King or Michael Jordan, you have plenty of fans eager to buy your book(s). For most of us, it is best to plan from the start to leverage our book and "published author" status to boost our business or other income-producing efforts, and the good news is there are hundreds of ways to do that.

Once your book is published, even if your original strategy or goal was not about its sales revenue, it may make sense to let Amazon and other booksellers offer your book for sale. After all, with the eBook version, you don't have to print and keep inventory, advertise to customers, take money or ship one single book! That's why it's called a "passive" income stream. Are you writing your book to create a passive income stream for yourself? If so, you need to make certain that you include as many reader benefits and features as you can that will make the book attractive for customers frequenting popular online book stores such as Amazon and Barnes & Noble. In a later chapter we'll show you how to get these shoppers' attention, starting with your book title.

Who Needs You?

As you are thinking about your book, it is critical to ask yourself who you have in mind as your target reader. Try to envision them as precisely as possible and keep them in your mind's eye as you plan and write. What topics do you think they will expect and want you to cover as they read your book? What problems do they have for which you can offer solutions? It is true that their expectations, by definition, have been conditioned by what they have read in the past on similar topics. Yet, no one has written *your* book, with *your* insights and intentions — you have a different take on the topic and different knowledge to convey. Nevertheless, reader expectations cannot be ignored because they must not only be met, but surpassed, to generate outstanding reviews of your book.

How Will The Reader Use Your Book?

Another consideration as you begin to develop your book in your mind is how your target reader is likely to use your book. Will he be using it as a general introduction to a topic? Will she be using it to acquire the necessary knowledge to employ a professional to accomplish one of her important goals, perhaps to hire an attorney to represent her in a family matter, or to select an accountant to do her taxes? Will he be using your book as a detailed how-to guide to create his own will, or to set up accounting software for his small business? Will she be using your book to avoid mistakes as she makes a big decision in her life such as choosing an investment advisor or seeking a specialist to consult about her particular health issue? Do you picture your reader as having an urgent problem looking for quick answers from an expert?

If you put yourself in your likely reader's shoes and answer the questions which cover the topics you think he will be looking for, you are preparing yourself to generate and capture relevant ideas which can be developed into a well-received and successful book.

Ask Yourself "What Can I Do To Set Myself Apart?"

Other than being coherent and well-written, the most important thing which impacts the success of your book is how well your chosen topic matches what readers are looking for. Since common sense tells us, then, to write about highly popular subjects, how would a reader find and decide to buy our particular book among the masses? The answer deserves careful consideration: Your book must be *different*. It actually is not as challenging as you may first think, given that you, your background, your perspectives and learned lessons ARE unique…no doubt about it. You simply need to spend some time identifying how your book can best be written, positioned, and titled in a unique way. Here are a few questions to ask yourself:

- What can I do with this topic to set myself apart?
- What makes me stand out in this area already?
- What do people ask me for advice about?
- What do my clients love about me?
- What are my skills I enjoy using the most?
- What issues are competitors ignoring?
- Where are the information or solution gaps?

Three Converging Circles Are Your Keys to Unlock A Hit Topic for Your Book

Your most-likely-to-succeed book topic will be one which you can expertly write about, genuinely care about, and which has a large enough, sufficiently interested audience. Whether writing an article, book, or speech, you probably already know how important being credible is for a nonfiction author. The surest route to credibility is to write about *what you know and what your credentials and experiences have prepared you to do.* If you follow that route, it is very likely that every page in your book will be effective in enhancing your reputation as an authority, rather than diminishing it.

Within the billions of bits of knowledge in your mind are many topics you could legitimately write about, and within these are ones **you actually care about**. This is where your motivation really begins to come into its own.

Narrow down your potential topics by filtering out any which bore you. A bored writer bores the reader as well as him/herself. An enthused writer has the energy to see the book project all the way through and will attract and keep the readers' attention more effectively.

Of course, the real success of your book depends on having a book people want to read. If you want your book to be both satisfying to write and successful in the marketplace (whether it is sold or given away to attract more business), your topic must be something your **audience cares about right now**. Topics which meet all three criteria are your sure-fire winners.

How To Choose Your Ideal Book Topic

Now you know the three things that successful writers keep in mind when they choose a topic. So how do you do it? Draw these three circles, fill them in with what you know, what excites you, and what your market research reveals. Look for the overlap — the center circle sweet spot.

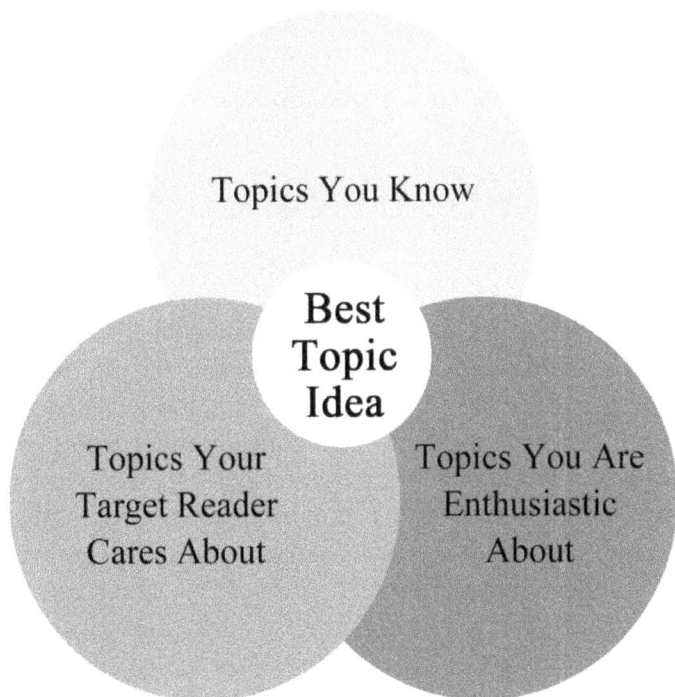

A great topic is one which you are enthusiastic to write about, have the credibility to do so, and have researched the market to know there are readers very eager to read what you have to share.

Why Two Out Of Three Is Never Good Enough

Many, many people have been thinking about writing a book for a long time. When you are ready to get serious, that book topic that has been percolating in you will naturally be the first one for you to consider. Then it's time to evaluate if all three criteria for a *successful* book topic are met by your topic idea. Often this is not the case, at least initially.

Let's look at a topic which has two out of three of the key criteria. One author started with the idea for writing a book about her experience coaching high-school girls' basketball. She took the team to the state finals two years in a row, and for years she organized her entire life around her passion for the game, and for teaching young women all she had to share about basketball and life.

However, when she really looked at her goals for publishing a book, her desired rewards for investing herself and her time in writing the book, she found she very much wanted one of her outcomes to be financial success – a considerable passive income stream. Her topic idea covered something of which she had first-hand knowledge and experience, and certainly she had authentic enthusiasm, but her story about a no-name team (the team did not go on to win the state championship) simply had too small a readership potential to reach her goal for book sales revenue. Her market research informed her that, fairly or unfairly, her stories were not about young *men's* basketball, and thus her characters were not likely to become NBA stars, and that this would dampen reader appeal. She could not count on enough demand and sufficient market share with her stories, and realized she could only expect some of her local school's supporters, her friends and family to buy the book.

A coach herself, she accepted the coaching illustrated in this chapter and went to work to fill in the missing piece. To have three out of three book topic criteria present and accounted for became her pre-writing goal. It was a great way to focus her intention to write a book with good sales potential. Now, she is currently in the process of writing her book, with its ideal book topic, on how twelve highly successful real-life women (including CEOs, MDs, and PhDs) attribute their competitive skills, team building and leadership excellence to early foundational skills and attitudes they built by playing high school sports. Her own stories and wisdom which she originally wanted to share are also included and fit in perfectly. Clearly, her chances for a successful book have been greatly expanded by this transformation.

Another two-out-of-three book topic example is the book a well-respected Dietitian wrote about a very effective and brilliantly simple approach to changing counterproductive habits and eating better as part of a healthier lifestyle. The expertise is there, the market is there, but the book fell as flat as a gluten-free pancake. The author simply did not have sufficient enthusiasm for the topic and it showed in the book. It entered the marketplace with a yawn and still sleeps there, unnoticed.

Still another common mistake is to choose a topic which has a hot market and excites your inner author, but is not something you know more than a few pages to write about. Here, the missing piece can be fixed fairly easily through research, learning, and leveraging the expertise of true gurus. We've all seen books which are actually just collected stories and wisdom of different experts, bookended with an introduction and conclusion by the "author" and, when published, took off on the fast track to being best-sellers. If you are burning with the passion to produce a book with a compelling theme or message, or following a hot trend, it is perfectly okay to enroll others and use their credentials to make it a three-out-of-three hit topic.

By listing the many interests you have which excite you, noting your own life experiences and education, and really listening to your target reader, you can fill in all three circles (in the above diagram) and see any topic's strengths and weaknesses. Then you can work to fill in all three essential elements to provide you with your best book topic choice.

Research shows that there are four categories which encompass the majority of popular nonfiction books: Health, wealth, relationships, and passions/hobbies. Even if the book topic which emerged in your three-circle process is not particular to one of these subjects, you may find a tie-in. If you decide to write about electric vehicles, for example, it would be wise to tout the cost-savings over time that EV owners enjoy from not having to spend their paycheck at the gas station. If your expertise on your topic enables you to provide people real guidance on how to improve some aspect of their health, wealth, relationships or passion, you will find an eager market.

Key Distinctions For This Chapter

All Three Topic Criteria vs. One or Two   A book may enjoy some level of success if it is at least what the reading audience cares about, or shines brightly with the author's authentic passion for the subject, or is packed with useful knowledge, but at the intersection of all three lies the ideal book topic.

Sourcing vs. Laboring   You are the source of your book's topic, message, tone, scope and purpose. If you choose, others can do the labor of outlining, writing, editing, formatting, publishing and/or marketing. Don't miss out on becoming a published author because you may not have the time, skills or desire to work through every step yourself.

Commit vs. Contemplate   When you commit, you start taking actions consistent with that commitment. If you say you are committed but there is no accompanying, measurable action, it is just wishful contemplation. Committed actions produce results.

Summary

The decision to write a book is a declaration that you have something to say that other people want to hear. When you start your book, **make a promise to yourself** that you can and will finish it. In a recent survey we conducted by polling a group of professional speakers, all were in agreement that "everyone has a book inside." Yet relatively few let it out.

Some people have been going along thinking:

1. I don't have a compelling story to share.

2. I don't know how to organize and write a book.

3. I just don't have time.

Well, just in the US last year, almost 300,000 new book titles were published, all written by people who had the *same* or *similar* thoughts, yet wrote and published a book

Remember the famous quote by Woody Allen? During an interview when discussing his advice to young writers, Allen said, "Eighty percent of success is showing up." You have what you need to write and publish a book: your experience, motivation to reach your goals, and resources to assist you with any part of the journey where your map isn't clear. Sometimes the hardest part is the beginning. When you utilize this chapter's three-criteria tool and discover what you are passionate about, and what your target reader is eager to learn which you already know, you will be off to a great start.

Chapter III

What Is The Right Length For Your EBook?

Pages And Dynamic Elements Matter

Understanding Length Choice For The EBook Version Of Your Book

When President John F. Kennedy boldly announced that the U.S.A. would put a man on the moon, he quoted a Confucian proverb that says "A journey of a thousand miles begins with a single step." You have taken a giant step toward being a published author by using the previous chapters to decide what you are going to write about. But now there are more steps to take. Few are more crucial than deciding how long your eBook will become before you declare it finished.

What should your length goal be? There is no simple answer. Even if you narrow the question to "How long should a business book be that covers my topic?" there are still no tried and true formulas for what is the "correct" length. But there are a few definitions, considerations, and publishing traditions that will help you decide.

There are nonfiction eBooks that are well worth reading with as few as 25 pages, especially if the eBook is on a technical subject that interests specialists and it is dense with statistics, charts, graphs and video or audio. These dynamic elements (which we discuss at length in a later chapter about making your eBook sing and dance) carry a lot of the message and so fewer pages of worded explanation are needed.

On the other hand, some college textbooks converted to an eBook format run over many hundreds of pages, plus a score or more of pages of footnotes and an index. Of course, these two extremes are at the far ends of the normal curve for eBooks.

Neither is right nor wrong. In fact there is a lively debate among book bloggers and the publishing community about what constitutes appropriate length for an eBook.

For example, in *How Many Pages Should a Nonfiction eBook Be?* Lance Winslow (EZine.com) writes, "Have you ever downloaded an eBook and …noted it was only 26 pages double-spaced with pictures, I mean come on–the Dr. Seuss books have more information in them. You call that an e-Book, please …you are kidding, right?"

"An eBook could be fifteen pages, but I've seen sales letters that long, and by the time you put in the graphics and pictures, table of contents, well, that's not an eBook, it is just a big beautiful brochure."

In Winslow's opinion, "An eBook ought to be at least 60-pages minimum including a table of contents, title page and index or reference page. If it is less than that, it's not really a book, it's just information in a mini-book format. …eBooks should be 60-120 pages, and for some more specific niche topics that encompass a large subject they can be longer of course."

Glen Ford, on the other hand, writes in his Ezinearticles.com article *Book Length – Average Length Of A Nonfiction Book,* "One of the questions that new writers always ask is 'How long should my nonfiction book be?'…However, part of the reason that new writers find it difficult to pin down an answer is because the answer is so difficult. It isn't as straightforward as it seems."

"…while the topic will have a great deal of influence, there are many other elements you need to take into account. Many of these are marketing related."

In principle, we agree with Ford. There is no hard and fast answer to how long a good business book should be. First, you need to establish a standard length of a page. Nonfiction typically has longer sentences and less white space because it doesn't have dialogue. 300 to 500 words are sometimes used as the yardstick, although 250 is also used, but like all the numbers when discussing book length, you should consider them as yardsticks rather than firm numbers.

Take a look in your business book library. You will find that almost all your books are more than 100 pages long (about 25,000 - 50,000 words depending on style.)

Many nonfiction books (usually business or self-help) have around 50 thousand words. If you are typing your manuscript as a standard 8.5" x 11" sized document, double-spaced, using a 12 point font, that will require around 200 pages, assuming each page has approximately 250 words.

There are two significant differences that affect length between eBooks and printed books, and there are several criteria to consider that will help you zoom in on an appropriate length for your eBook.

The differences are simple but significant.

Because eBooks are digital and are meant to be displayed on an electronic device screen, they are free from the "tyranny of the press" and "signatures" which are the printed and folded sheets used to make a bound book. This gives the person who lays the book out (whether it is the author or a graphic designer working for a publisher) a lot more flexibility.

EBooks have the capacity to be dynamic. We explore this fully in Chapter IX, *Dynamic EBooks, Making Your Manuscript Sing and Dance*. Basically, a dynamic eBook (DEB) is an eBook that has its content enriched with state-of-the-art multimedia technology that becomes a high-tech way of communicating ideas. An "enhanced eBook" (EEB) is the same thing.

Creating a DEB goes beyond simply digitizing the printed page. As the next step of eBook evolution, it leverages existing technology as a powerful idea messenger. Done right, it dramatically increases the sheer communicating power and impact of a page in an eBook. Enhancements to the reading experience are rapidly becoming as expected in the marketplace as high-definition television has become.

So, as you consider how long your eBook manuscript should be, you do not have to take into consideration the technological and economic constraints of conventional book printing. It need only be long enough to get your ideas across to your intended audience and not one word more. One author reported that he saw the width of the spine of his paperback book first run sample, went back to his manuscript and added 45 pages of what he called "fluff" and republished and printed the book, simply because he felt his book had looked too thin — a consideration an eBook author or reader would never have!

Best of all, if you plan to create an enhanced eBook, as you outline and write your manuscript you know your words and photos do not have to carry the entire load of communication for your ideas. Dynamic elements are very content-rich and if a picture is worth a thousand words, think how many words you can incorporate into a video clip that only takes up a fraction of a page.

Factors Affecting eBook Length

Genre. Each genre of book has a conventional length that does not have to be strictly adhered to, but affects audience expectations and possibly reviews. For example, fiction works are usually longer than nonfiction. Anthologies are usually longer than books by a single author as they contain the ideas of many contributors and are expected to be a comprehensive representation of the topic.

Subject. Since we are focusing on nonfiction eBooks, the "right" or "appropriate" length of your manuscript is likely to be 100-200 pages. Besides the amount of dynamic content (the more dynamic content, the shorter the manuscript tends to be — but does not have to be), a main driver affecting length is subject matter. A book explaining how a search algorithm affects traffic to your web site, for example, is likely to be information-dense and fairly short. On the other hand, a book about marketing a web site would probably be longer.

Size of the page or font Usually your eBook will be laid out like a standard paperback book, six-by-nine inches, but you have total flexibility with digital publishing. You can even have more than one sized version like one client decided to do with his gourmet cooking eBook – his decision based on market research. Predetermined page size, page breaks, and type style and size in an eBook are optional, and such eBooks are called "fixed layout," whereas "reflowable" eBooks allow the reader to change the font size (affecting the quantity of "pages") and control other options for a customized reading experience.

Size of competitors' printed books. While you should definitely take a field trip to your local brick-and-mortar or online book store and locate and identify the size of competitive print books, you should keep in mind our observations that these are more often dictated by the requirements of printing presses and the economics of the book market than the ideal length. What people observe in book stores about book length on a given topic often unconsciously forms expectations of how long a particular type of book should be. However, eBooks are changing reader expectations quickly as more and more people turn to digital publications.

Size of competitive eBooks. The size of similar eBooks (as determined by a thorough search of online eBook stores) is more of a relevant criterion than printed books, but it still should not control how long your manuscript must be. Since many of the current crop of eBooks are simply digitally-formatted versions of conventional print books, they often reflect the length considerations of printed books that we have discussed. Also, since dynamic eBooks are relatively new in the marketplace, they have not yet had anywhere near the effect they are bound to have on reader expectations of expected size. As DEBs become the norm, we predict that eBook size will shrink rather than grow.

The character of your dynamic elements. The number and size of dynamic elements in your eBook manuscript can have a significant impact on its length. The more that you use dynamic elements to accent and extend your descriptions, definitions, and illustrations of key points, the less words of explanation will be needed. Clearly, words still matter mightily in a book, even a DEB, but they don't have to carry the entire load. The need for good writing is not repealed by dynamic content. You'll still need to outline your book carefully and craft effective sentences to introduce and describe topics, and provide some perspective to their contextual meaning within your DEB manuscript.

Good and tightly-integrated writing affects perceived length. If your book is well-written and you and your editor have developed prose that is both easy to read and well-integrated with the dynamic elements in your eBook, its apparent or perceived length will be longer, perhaps much longer, than actual word count indicates. In other words, because of the great editing *and* the tight integration of your book's dynamic elements and words, the reading experience should be equivalent to a much longer book and far richer too.

EBook Types And Target Lengths

Evaluating all of the factors that affect eBook length allows us to classify eBooks into types and to suggest target lengths for each. Two caveats are in order for this taxonomy. First, this and any classification of book types is arbitrary. Because of that, other analysts may have different terms for the same or similar concepts.

Secondly, the target lengths are equally arbitrary and should be taken as the center of a range of acceptable lengths. Think of the range we suggest for each type as the center section of a bell curve. Most of the instances of eBooks of a given type will fall within the center section of the curve, but outliers exist and should not be dismissed as "wrong" because of length alone.

Amazon, the world's largest bookseller, utilizes this concept very effectively when they embrace a type of short eBook and describe what they call "Kindle Singles" as "…the highest-quality work we can find, and at a length best suited to the ideas they present…compelling ideas expressed at their natural length— writing that doesn't easily fall into the conventional space limitations of magazines or print books. Kindle Singles are typically between 5,000 and 30,000 words."

David Carnoy said in a CNET article in January, 2011 that "You'd think 'Kindle Singles' was the name for a new online dating service for Kindle owners. But it's really a new category in the Kindle Store that features written works longer than a typical magazine article, or as much as a few chapters of a typical book."

White Paper EBook

A "White Paper" is what Wikipedia calls "an authoritative report or guide that helps solve a problem…used to educate readers and help people make decisions..."

Originally a term applied to public policy documents, now White Papers have become widespread in business. They often are the preferred form for marketing essays that promote a given product or process, or provide useful background information.

For our purpose of discussing nonfiction eBooks, a White Paper eBook:

Is usually a monograph on a given subject.

Is intended to inform the reader about a topic, or, to promote a product or process.

Usually includes many charts, graphs, hyperlinks and other dynamic elements.

Falls with the customary length of between 20 and 50 pages or 5,000 to 12,500 words, using the arbitrary allocation of 250 words on a page.

Short EBook

A Short eBook, similar to a White Paper eBook in length but usually different in scope, is:

Typically not constrained by adherence to a single topic like a monograph.

For nonfiction, intended to cover a subject by including not only facts but the author's opinions, related personal stories, and many times a message or lesson(s).

A common form for business eBooks, but also used for other genres including short stories, novellas and even poetry.

An eBook, if intended for a business audience, usually containing some dynamic elements, but typically not as many as a White Paper since there is room within it for well-chosen words to carry more of the explanatory load.

An eBook, in this context, that is intended to explain a complex or confusing topic to clients or potential clients.

An eBook falling within a customary length of between 25 and 60 pages, or 10,000 to 15,000 words, using the arbitrary 250 words on a page.

Medium EBook (Typical)

A medium eBook is very similar to a short eBook but it is, in the simplest terms, longer. We define it as:

Not usually constrained by adherence to a single topic.

Intended to cover a reasonably comprehensive topic and explore a subject with some depth. For example, a medium eBook might be an introduction to wills and trusts or, for a physician, a complete guide to living with allergies.

A common length for business eBooks, but also the most popular length for Kindle Singles, memoirs, how-to books, workbooks, poetry collections, and so forth.

Falling within the customary length of between 60 and 100 or more pages or 15, 250 to 50,000 words or longer.

Long EBook

A long eBook is not yet as common as shorter electronic publications. Longer eBooks are, like all categories of eBooks, increasing in availability. They are typically:

Intended to provide an in-depth treatment of a subject.

Published as new electronic versions of existing long books, especially biographies, reference, and text books.

Often college-level text books; but eBooks are beginning to replace bulky, quickly outdated and expensive hard-cover printed text books at all grade levels.

Comprehensive and have incorporated dynamic elements, especially video, to enhance a student's learning, or, in a biography, to bring the subject to life.

Over 100 pages, and sometimes over 1000 pages.

How Long Should My eBook Be?

Length	Typical Page Range	Common Examples
Short	25-59	• Many Children's Books • Some Scientific Papers
Medium	60-100 pages	• Most Business eBooks • How-to Guides
Long	101 pages To Over 1,000	• Biographies • Some Text Books

Knowing When To Say "Good — Enough!" A Checklist:

The cliché that "perfect" is the enemy of "good" certainly applies to eBook manuscripts. Knowing when you are done with a book is not strictly adhering to a set of marketplace   expectations or conforming to admittedly arbitrary formulas for length.

Frankly, knowing when to say "my book is done" is essentially an editorial judgment about its quality and whether your words, illustrations, and dynamic elements have accomplished their task of clearly presenting your ideas and information to the reader.

The following checklist should help give you confidence that you really do know when your book is good, and enough, and **it's time to publish**.

☐ I stuck to my outline when I wrote the book.

☐ I have made all the important points in my outline and few extraneous points.

☐ I have checked major online bookstores and determined the range of length of competitive eBooks with and without dynamic elements, and used that as a rough guide to reader and publisher expectations.

☐ My manuscript is of conventional length for the topic, taking into account that my dynamic elements may allow for a shorter word content without affecting the "apparent length." If it is an outlier with respect to length, I have good reason for it to be so.

☐ My ideas on the topic of this single stand-alone eBook, or an eBook that is part of a series, are focused rather than wandering off into other distantly related but not germane topics.

☐ I see that I have many more ideas that are related to the general subject of my manuscript, but are probably dissimilar enough that they should be the subject of their own eBook rather than being part of this particular eBook.

□ I have asked a few people in my target market to read the book and none of them answered "yes" to the questions of whether it was too short or too long.

□ My editor agrees that all excessive verbiage and long-winded sentences have been wrung-out of the manuscript.

□ Any dynamic elements I have created are well-supported by, and integrated into, the prose that surrounds them.

□ I have chosen good insertion locations in the manuscript where dynamic elements can convey relevant, useful information to add value to the readers' experience.

Key Distinctions For This Chapter

Length Range vs. Length Rule   There are no set rules or constraints, only expectations that an eBook's length justifies it being categorized as a "book" but not so long that it burdens or bores the reader. An eBook should be easy to consume, is typically between 100 and 200 pages, and if too long it can easily be converted into two or more eBooks.

Dynamic Elements vs. Words Only   Multimedia features such as video and audio which are embedded in an eBook affect the length of the book. They could replace whole paragraphs of words, shortening the number of pages, or, if the elements are added in throughout an existing manuscript, the eBook would be expanded in length.

Market-driven vs. Conventional   What do readers want and expect? Today this is the key consideration when determining the length of your eBook, not the outdated parameters regarding printed book page size and length.

Summary

While there is no absolute rule for the right size for an eBook, or any book, there are many conventions, reader expectations, and practices that help authors decide upon length.

EBooks, particularly those with dynamic elements such as video and audio, tend to be shorter than those without them, but in some cases the number of pages increases.

EBooks can be arbitrarily divided into White Papers, Short or Medium eBooks, and Long eBooks. No matter which form you choose, it is important to let the subject matter and reader expectations control the length of your book rather than any arbitrary classification.

Chapter IV

Book Titles

How To Write Powerful, Magnetic Titles And Subtitles

Stand Out Among Thousands Of Competitors: A Title Is Your Billboard

Do you judge whether you're going to invest time or money in something based on its name, reputation, or title, at least, initially? We all do.

That's one of the reasons why choosing the *title* of your book with care is very important to your book's success. The cliché that people judge a book by its cover has a basis in fact, and your title is a major component of your cover. A creative, catchy title can significantly increase the number of people who can find your book in an online search, and who will take interest in your book and maybe even recommend it to others.

A title that is both catchy *and* key word optimized can serve as a powerful magnet to draw in your target readers. Key word optimized is often called SEO (**Search Engine Optimized**) which means certain words are used precisely because search engines such as Google have statistics indicating these words have high volumes of people using these words when searching the Internet for a topic. It is critical to identify the words and phrases (a "key word" can also mean a phrase containing several words) most often associated with your book topic.

According to Jay Conrad Levinson, the "Guerilla Marketing Guru," at least half of a book's success is attributable to the title. Choosing your title with care and consideration based on proven marketing principles is one of the most worthwhile things you can do as an author.

A good way to start is by keeping a few important things in mind as you brainstorm and research your optimum book title: What crosses the mind of a potential reader who sees a book title? Most people automatically consider "What's in it for me? Do I want or need to read this?" This means that having a *benefit* in your title is a good idea. Also, the title ought to be what the movie industry calls "high concept" which is something you grasp and connect with immediately. The message for the reader must be concise and have instant impact. **You have just eight seconds to capture a browsing reader's attention**.

Make sure that your title (with subtitle) accurately describes the unique selling proposition (USP) of your book. In other words, what unique information (or benefit) is your book offering? Once you answer that for yourself, integrate it into your title. For example, *MS Windows for Dummies* immediately tells the browsing reader they don't have to already know anything about MS Windows to get started using that book. If you are a beginner and want to know how to use Windows on your computer, you instantly relate to the message of that title; it's attractive to you because you can quickly recognize it as a good match.

Subtitles: Can A Book Live Without One?

A subtitle is highly recommended for two reasons. First, it can communicate additional compelling benefit(s) found in your book because it doesn't need to be short (i.e., three to five words) like the main title. The short, catchy title sells a prospective reader on reading the subtitle which can then provide a sense of "what's in this for me?" Secondly, a well-written subtitle is saturated with SEO key words. It will be a beacon to target readers searching your topic on the Internet. Let's look at an eBook previously published by one of this book's authors: The title of *Words @ Work* is extended and explained by the subtitle, *A Business Writing Handbook For The Internet-Savvy.*

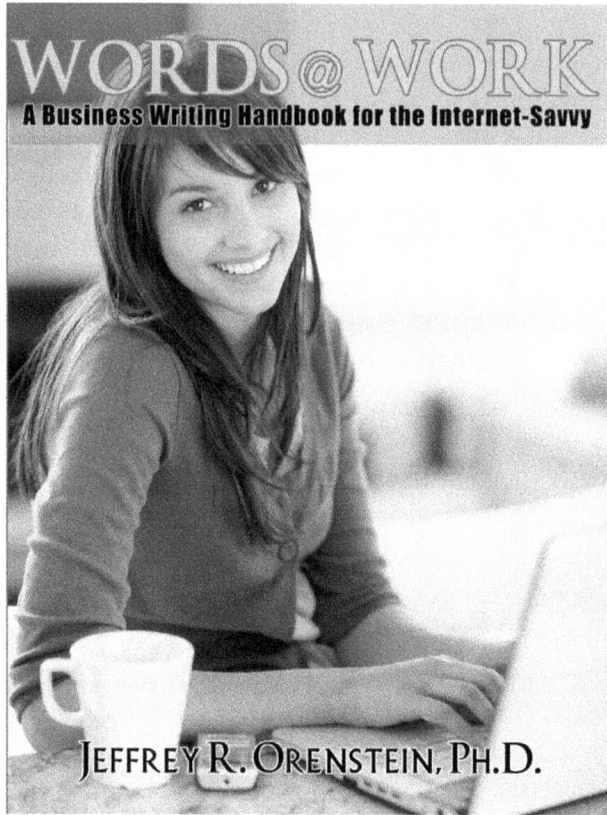

WORDS @ WORK
A Business Writing Handbook for the Internet-Savvy

JEFFREY R. ORENSTEIN, PH.D.

What Problem Are You Going To Solve?

What problem are you going to solve for your reader? How will reading your book benefit your target reader? Try this title formula to help you with your positioning:

How to _____ So you can _____

This is not necessarily the format of your title, but it helps you clarify what you want your book title to communicate. Don't write *features* — write *benefits*!

Your book title needs to be what your target readers are looking for or what they really need whether they know it or not. You may have some amazing ideas to share, but they will not reach their full readership potential unless you always try to answer the "so what?" in your reader's mind. By emphasizing benefit(s) in this way, people will see **how** what you are offering will be valuable and helpful.

Sometimes a very appealing title emphasizes a change you promise for your readers. A good example is *Why People Don't Heal and How They Can*, by Carolyn Myss. Another one is *The Luck Factor – Change Your Luck and Change Your Life*, by Richard Wiseman.

How Are You Going To Get Their Attention?

It's also a good idea to create a book title that arouses curiosity for potential readers. A great title will naturally trigger questions in the mind of those who see it and be an inducement to find answers to what they want to know. *Journeys To Abstraction: 100 Paintings and Their Secrets Revealed*, by Sue St. John, is a provocative title for those readers interested in the "secrets" behind the art featured in this book.

Arousing curiosity serves to draw your potential audience in to give your book a try. And, like "secrets revealed," the title needs to let people know their questions will be answered when they read your book. The late, great, leadership guru, Steven Covey, is known for his bestseller, *The Seven Habits of Highly Effective People*. Upon seeing this title, most of us start to wonder what makes people highly effective and, because we are told by the title that it is seven particular habits, we assume we'll find out about those habits in this book. Then we too will have the keys to being highly effective.

Notice the title does not just say *The Habits*…but gives a certain number. This is very common in nonfiction and how-to books because a number gives added emphasis, and it tells readers what to expect. If the reader is looking for efficiency and ease, they will pick up *The 5 Easy Steps to Conquering Clutter* more often than *The Complete Guide to Getting Your Home Organized*. Sometimes a large number is best to use as it gives an abundance of hope, solutions, or encouragement: *200 Ways to Promote Your Book For Free*. Using a number to indicate a time frame can be especially attractive in some instances: *How To Sell Your Home in 60 Days, Guaranteed*.

Great Title vs. Good Title

How can you know precisely which words or phrases to use in your title? Start with a list of SEO potential words to use. Draft some three-to-five-word title ideas and ask yourself:

When said out loud, does it sound good to me?

Does it use words which are easy for your target reader to understand and pronounce?

Does it use alliteration? (repeating sounds or words) e.g. *Get Organized, Get Published*, or, *Dog People's Guide to Perfect Pup Manners.*

Does it have active verbs? Words which end with –*ing* are often used. e.g. *Spontaneous Healing* by Dr. Andrew Weil. Another example: *Thank You, Mrs. McCormack: 5 Steps to Capturing Kids' Hearts* by Paul J. Meyer.

Does it evoke an emotion? Will the reader feel more confident, less sad, more lucky?

Verbs are crucial. Legendary advertising giant, Leo Burnett, set out to define what made some ads successful and what caused others to fail. According to Burnett, "Dull and exaggerated ad copy is due to the excess use of adjectives." His extensive research of failed ads and highly successful messages (such as Lincoln's *Gettysburg Address*) concluded: Use more verbs, not adjectives. Verbs increase the pulling-power and believability of ad copy, speeches, book titles and sales letters. Mr. Burnet compiled a list of the most persuasive verbs.

108 Power Verbs For Making a Good Title (or Subtitle) Great

Abolish Accelerate Achieve Act Adopt Align Anticipate Apply Assess Avoid

Boost Break Bridge Build Burn

Capture Change Choose Clarify Comprehend Confront Connect Conquer Convert Create Cross

Decide Define Defuse Deliver Deploy Design Develop Diagnose Discover Drive

Eliminate Ensure Establish Evaluate Exploit Explore

Filter Finalize Find Focus Foresee

Gain Gather Generate Grasp

Identify Ignite Illuminate Implement Improve Increase Innovate Inspire Intensify

Lead Learn Leverage

Manage Master Maximize Measure Mobilize Motivate

Overcome Penetrate Persuade Plan Position Prepare Prevent Profit

Raise Realize Reconsider Reduce Refresh Replace Resist Respond Retain

Save Scan Segment Shatter Shave-off Sidestep Simplify Solve Stimulate Stop Stretch Succeed Supplement

Take Train Transfer Transform Understand Unleash Use Whittle-down Win

Pay attention to television, print, and online advertising that you like, as well as to advertising that turns you off, because we can learn a lot by scrutinizing both effective and unappealing advertising. Whenever you begin to draft your book title, sales letter, website, blog post, video book trailer script, or email campaign, or otherwise discuss your features and benefits, use verbs from the list above. Remember, your customer wants to know "What will this book do for me?" and these power verbs are proven to put the pulling action into your communications.

Key Words

We live in a virtual shopping age where people increasingly search for books, especially eBooks, online rather than gazing at book spines on shelves at book stores or libraries. This is why the parts of your title which come up in the many search engine results should be researched carefully and placed in your title with precision for best results. The key is to ask yourself if your title contains key words that people are actually looking for. If you choose your title well, it will be something that a large segment of your target market will easily find via a search engine when they are looking for solutions and information on your topic. This search could be via an Internet browser, but it also could be performed on a particular web site such as Amazon.

Amazon does not have a specific tool to check key words, but it does have an auto-populate tool which means common phrases show up in a drop-down box when the beginning of an associated word is typed in. For example, if in the Kindle store search box you type "career," a list will appear which contains the most likely phrases you may be interested in: "career change," "career coaching," "career choices," "career change after 40," etc.

Google is, by far, the most used Internet search engine. Often the person who googles key words is not necessarily looking for a *book*, but when your title shows up in the search results, they are excited to find an entire book, not just a related article or a mention in a blog. The more people who see your title, the more your ideas are exposed to a wider audience who can become aware of the potential benefits of your information and ideas.

How Long Is A Great Title?

As you are asking yourself if your initial idea for a title sounds good to you, remember that it should not be too long. Short titles are effective because they are easy to take in at a glance and are easy to remember. For nonfiction, the goals of your title include clearly describing what is in your book, stating the main benefits for the reader, and including some key words people are searching for. The trick to accomplishing these seemingly contradictory goals (short, yet descriptive, SEO, and benefit-oriented) is simple: incorporate all of these criteria by creating a short title and coupling it with a longer subtitle.

Picture your future book cover, or a cover for a book titled *Simplify Your Life: A Six Week Plan to Clear Out Everything in Your Home and Life Which No Longer Nurtures You*. The words "Simplify Your Life" would appear in a large font. The book cover icons on Internet sites like Amazon are very small (and are called "thumbnails") and if your title is not large and bold it cannot be read by looking at the cover. Book cover icons appear even smaller on the now ubiquitous smart phones. Your subtitle, however, can be in a much smaller font, and can be much longer. When search engines "see" your book, they see all the words in both the title and subtitle and will pick up the many key words included in both with no consideration for type size.

Another advantage to having a short title is you will want to own an Internet domain name for your book. Example: Our client chose this SEO (search engine optimized) title: *The Insurer's Handbook: The Complete Cost-Cutting Guide to Moving Cases to Closure.* Once decided, he quickly reserved the domain name TheInsurersHandbook.com. A co-author of this book has a book selling on Amazon with the title *It's Okay, Ginger: A Story of Reassurance for Children When Parents Divorce.* She owns the domain name ItsOkayGinger.com.

Key Words + Magnetic Charge = Powerfully Attractive, Great Title

Other than imagining yourself in your target readers' shoes, how do you choose what key words are most important to include in your title if you want search engines to find you when they should? How can you be sure each word performs well in its job to attract readers?

First, let's see what the best-selling titles are in your book category. Go to the Amazon.com book site and Barnes & Noble.com and search for your book type by category and topic. Sort by popularity and see which books are top sellers. Obviously these books are like magnets, drawing readers and having them buy based on what they imagine and expect to find. It is as if these titles are magnetically charged. During your research, notice which titles you feel drawn to. Why? Do many of the top sellers use the same word? If so, chances are good that the common word is probably an effective key word that is optimized for search results.

Don't be discouraged if you find a huge number of book titles similar to your chosen title. That is good news rather than bad news! It is a great clue that people are past needing to be educated and already know that they need and want books on your topic. Since people are already buying that kind of book, you know there is a market niche for it that you can respond to with your unique approach.

If you cannot pinpoint your book category or are stuck on a title even after carefully looking at similar top-selling books in your niche, do not get discouraged. Another smart action is to look at the titles of any top-selling books and observe what appeals to you. Perhaps you can use one of these successful titles as a model for your book title. When naming her workbook about restocking and organizing one's kitchen to support a healthy lifestyle, one of our co-authors decided on *The Purpose-Driven Kitchen* which borrows recognition from Rick Warren's *The Purpose-Driven Life* – a book with over 30 million copies sold!

Now let's get a little technical. There are a lot of statistics readily available to you about what words people are using for search terms on the Internet. You don't have to guess: tools such as Wordtracker and Google Ad Words are effective in tracking this critical information.

Look under "tools" at the web site of SEO.com also you can try Google's keyword search tool in "AdWords." These research tools will help you focus in on your target.

It is a great idea to also use Google for your searches because it is the same resource over three million unique users go to every single day. Let's say you are a realtor writing a dynamic eBook for new homeowners to offer for free on your web site. When you type "homeowners" into the Google search bar, the automatic most-often-searched terms which begin with that word pop up. You may see "homeowners insurance" and "homeowners complaints" and "homeowners tax benefits" and "homeowners home warranties." These terms not only point you in the right direction to writing your book title and subtitle, they could easily be chapter names within your book – topics that you know already interest people even if they are not the main thrust of your book.

Now, here is a secret…while it would never occur to most people, the fact is that Amazon is the fourth largest search engine in the world. Its search function also can give you key words and phrases which millions of people are keying in, and the best part is, these are not just web surfers – they are buyers!

Pinpoint Your Person Of Interest (Your Target Reader)

Remember: Narrow is better in key word searches. The market could be saturated with books on your topic, so the more you narrow your focus the more people you will attract. Even though it sounds counterintuitive, it is not. Many authors assume incorrectly that catering to a very large audience will mean capturing more readers. Actually, narrow audience niches typically produce more results. The more you clearly pinpoint your ideal reader, the person who is most intensely interested in your topic and is motivated to search for information about it, the better your chances are of connecting with the people who will download or purchase your book because it is such a good match for them.

As a marketing strategy, this is effective because instead of trying to be convincing, you simply focus on **connecting with your niche**. The more narrowly you target, the easier your marketing task is because people are doing a lot of work for you by self-selecting. Your book title should make it easy for people to self-select. You want the most exposure to your target readers, and you want them to actually find you, and they only look for what is most relevant to their situation, interest or problem. Speaking of problems, there is a theory that to really nail the best topic and title you should address not just what you think (and confirm) a lot of people are interested in – you should write what they are *desperate* to know. These are your most highly qualified prospects, the ones most likely to take action once they find your book.

Find and Push Your Target Reader's Hot Button

How do you know what people are currently *desperate* to know? There is no better way to research this than to examine real questions from real people. Begin by finding related "forums" to discover the questions or problems which are reoccurring. To find a forum in your niche, you can start with a Google search of the name of your niche and the word "forum." Inside the forum, check out the "hot topics." Consider that each question could end up as a chapter in your book.

Similarly, you can find key questions and issues related to your topic by using a search engine to find related blogs. You will want to become familiar with the top five blogs in your niche. One more easy way to access what could be critical questions is to check the "answers" site at yahoo.com. Remember, you are mostly interested in the *questions*, not the answers, which could be incorrect, and certainly aren't to be used rather than your own. If you use these three simple research ideas you will have a much better grasp of what content your target readers are eager to consume.

Don't be surprised if you find so many related questions that you explode with ideas for content for your book. Not only could you use your research results to add chapters, you may decide to write an additional book! Here is an example to illustrate the point. If you are writing an eBook about training and caring for pets, and you have sufficient content and expertise to encompass both dogs and cats, it makes great marketing sense to write two eBooks instead of one. One could have "cats" in the title and the other could have "dogs" in the title, thereby appealing to cat lovers or dog lovers who are searching for information about their favorite domestic animal. By the way, the last chapter in each book could be effective at cross-marketing your books by briefly covering cats in the dog book, and dogs in the cat book, since a reader is often interested in both. Of course you will mention your other eBook which is almost entirely devoted to the companion topic. With an eBook, you can include the hyperlink as well.

There Are No Digital Stone Tablets – A Title Can Be Changed More Easily Than You Think

Do you realize how easy it is to test different titles or change a book title for an eBook? You can quickly put your eBook up for sale on eBay, for example, under two different titles, and see which one generates the most interest. Alternatively, you can give away one chapter and perhaps get more participation and accomplish your goal of seeing which title is more magnetic. Even after your eBook is published, you can change the title (or anything in the book) without much trouble since you will not have to discard an inventory of printed books and replace them with newer versions. Even with your printed and bound version, you can change your title or anything in your book and instantly have a new Print-on-Demand, revised edition produced one book at a time. This is one of the ways the publishing industry has undergone a transformative change which is so beneficial to you, the author.

One quick but usually helpful method to test your final three or four title options is to send an email out to your personal contacts, especially anyone who you think is a likely target reader for your book, and ask for their vote and ranking. Tools such as "Survey Monkey" are free and facilitate any market research you may need to conduct via the Internet. You can get valuable feedback as well as stir up interest in your project. One author felt confident about her book title but wanted to test three different subtitles. She received 22 replies, and her personal favorite subtitle received 20 first-choice votes — she felt validated and ready to finalize her title and move on.

Once you have a title which includes the right key words to help the right people find your book, you don't want to overthink this and thereby hold up the design of your book cover and other steps toward completing your project and getting published. Do the best you can to choose a great title and go with it, knowing it is not written in stone and can be modified later.

Key Distinctions for this Chapter

Title Qualities vs. Subtitle Qualities   Both should have clear, simple language, and include key words and phrases which target readers are using to search the Internet. A title should be short, usually under seven words. The subtitle can be more descriptive and use more than twice as many words. On the cover, the title should be in a large and easy-to-read font, and the (longer) subtitle can be in a smaller font. Both should contain strong verbs and few adjectives. Both should be benefit-oriented and designed to narrow and pinpoint the intended audience vs. being too general, wide and weak.

Benefit vs. Feature   A feature is an aspect of what you are offering, whereas a benefit is how what you are offering will help. A benefit-oriented title is a reader/customer-oriented title and is more magnetic. The reader is asking themselves, "What's this going to do for me?" and is looking for a stated benefit to try on and see if it fits. Strong persuasive verbs reinforce benefits. It's important to use both benefits and features in describing your book, but people generally buy on benefits and are reassured by features.

Desperate To Know vs. Browsing   Using the power and immediacy of the Internet, people with an urgent question will search for an instant answer or solution with a high level of motivation to acquire what they need. They will use certain words in their search criteria and these can be identified and used in a book title so that title is found and displayed. When the information is offered as an EBook available in multiple formats, it becomes easy for people to gain instant access to what they are seeking. Other people may come across your book and take interest, but these browsers are not nearly as likely to take action and download your book. The title should be a magnet for the most motivated searchers.

Summary

Developing and testing the title for your book is a critical step. Unless you are famous or spend a lot of money on advertising, most of your readers will find your book by searching the Internet, so you need your title words to match what your target audience is looking for. Next, the title must speak to and capture the potential reader by emphasizing a benefit they can expect. Use persuasive verbs and SEO key words in order to make your title (with its subtitle) a powerful magnet for your target readers. Take some extra time to test your title, but not so much time and overthinking that you delay your book and miss your publishing timeline goals.

Chapter V

Beginning The Writing Process

Steps To Advance Toward Your Goals

Listen To, And Trust Yourself: You Have All You Need To Write A Book

As discussed in previous chapters in this book, accomplishing your writing goals starts with your idea. Because your eventual outline will be your blueprint for the book you will write based on your idea, it makes sense to think like an architect as you start planning your book. Just as an architect develops an idea into a vision, and eventually, a set of drawings for a building, you as an author will develop your idea and build your book.

Upon receiving a project assignment, the architect thinks about it, applies his knowledge of building and design, and talks with the client and other stakeholders who will use the building. He/she considers the ways it will be used, where it will be located, how it should fit into the environment, the statement the finished product should make, and how large the building should be, among other variables.

As the architect of your eBook, you should consider some basic guidelines and proven approaches before you put pen to paper or place your fingers on a keyboard to start your book project.

The Idea Collection Process

When you brainstorm ideas, you are revisiting the idea collection process from a different vantage point; it's like when you open your clothes closet door wide and survey everything to see what inventory you already have. It can bring an important new awareness of things which had not been top of mind, and affect the direction your project needs to head. This stage is not about decision-making or option reduction, but instead is designed to elicit all ideas, including those which may not have been the first to come to mind, ideas which may have been hiding in the back of the closet, so to speak. Bringing them all out now is important.

"The best way to have a good idea is to have a lot of ideas."

– Linus Pauling

This is more of a right-brain activity, sparking the imaginative and non-editor side of your thinking. You need to give yourself a lot of creative license, and use a process that works well for you. Here are a few guidelines that many people find helpful to facilitate this early stage of book development:

1. To avoid shutting down your (right brain) creative side, use unlined paper. Also, it is best to use 11x17 or larger paper as you never know how big a brainstorm you may produce. Try turning the paper sideways or "landscape" because it may work better to let you see more of the page at one time.

2. Choose a comfortable writing instrument that you enjoy using, one which glides easily even when writing quickly. Use the same one throughout this process, as it is less disruptive than switching to different colors or other instruments.

3. Write the topic in the center and circle it, or quickly sketch a symbol representing the essence or theme of what you plan to write.

4. Set a timer for seven minutes, or just jot the ending time on the upper left corner as a reminder.

5. As quickly as possible, write as many ideas related to this topic as you can. Don't worry about organization or where they appear on your page. Use personal shorthand, abbreviations, symbols, or any other method you have for free-flow and fast writing. There is no right or wrong way to do this as long as you can remember what your marks and symbols mean, and they mean the same thing every time you use them. If you want to write an entire sentence that springs to mind, that is fine too. Collecting ideas is an art, not a science. Do not judge or edit what your hand wants to write – a seemingly random idea could later prove to be a key connection to your topic.

6. After the initial mental burst, take a short break. The connections and newly summoned ideas will start to build up in your mind again. After a few minutes, you can sit

down and take another five to seven minutes to record your thoughts as they freely flow.

7. If you still feel full of related ideas after your next break, you can make another pass at this idea collection process, or it may work better to put your paper aside and come back to it the next day. Jot down something if it occurs to you during the time between focused sessions.

8. You may use more than one piece of paper for your ideas. You may want to keep all your notes to mine for gems you can use in your next project. To keep moving forward with writing the particular book you are working on now, let's move on to the next phase which begins the organization and development of your captured ideas.

Categorizing Ideas

When you next sit down with your collection(s) of ideas, look for themes or categories which would naturally classify words or phrases into groups. In the clothes closet analogy, you would start sorting everything into "shirts," "slacks," "sweaters," and so forth. Sorting your ideas, as you begin to look for themes, you will also see that many of your ideas don't belong in the content scope of this particular book project…perhaps a future book is already germinating in your mind!

Exactly like the first step in any big organizing project, simplifying is a critical key to getting started on the right track. A person who wants to organize their closet should first reduce the number of items to organize by removing the seldom-worn and ill-fitting clothes and shoes. This simplification step is crucial to the success of subsequent steps. As you start organizing your ideas, a process sometimes referred to as "clustering," you will start to see which ideas belong or do not belong.

As you identify main themes, you can start notating which ideas belong in which category. You'll make a decision, then impose a highly visual designation. A quick way to do that is to draw a circle around all ideas related to the first theme, a triangle around ideas related to the second theme, etc. Another option is to use circles for all themes, but use different colored pens. You will then see at a glance how many ideas relate to each theme, which ideas don't belong and will not move on to the next step, and how that step is starting to shape up.

Writing a nonfiction book essentially involves packaging what you know and want to share in a way that is effectively organized for easy consumption. If your content is instructional, it should be organized in a way which encourages immediate application by your target readers. Therefore these steps of simplifying and clustering are essential in this early stage.

The Mind Map: Building The Bridge From Brainstorm To Book

What is mind-mapping? It is simply a tool to facilitate the step between listing an abundance of ideas and writing your outline. Mind-mapping is not the only way to bridge that gap, but you must somehow work through a method that simplifies, categorizes, and organizes your content. Like any map, a mind map shows a central topic, its key elements, and some level of detail within those elements. Because it represents the step in-between a burst of ideas and an actual written outline, it needs a purpose-driven framework and clear language.

Challenging Your Brain With Mind-Mapping

For a thorough explanation of mind-mapping and its many applications including strategic planning, refer to *The Mind Map Book* by Tony Buzon. For a single eBook-sized project, you should be able to utilize mind-mapping just by following our abbreviated guidelines in this book.

As recommended for the earlier step of idea collection, it is useful to work with a large piece of unlined paper, a flip chart, or a whiteboard. It is not uncommon for some mind-mapping processes to cover a large whiteboard – or you may simply want to have several large sheets of blank paper handy. In addition to giving yourself enough space, you want to give yourself a sufficient block of time, without distractions, and yet it works best to work quickly. Try to allocate between 10 and 25 minutes for the first pass at converting your free-range ideas into an organized format which depicts the relationships of the ideas you put on your map. Some mind-mappers like to sit down with paper while others strongly prefer to stand up and use a flip chart or white board.

Because you will be engaging both your right and left brain during mind-mapping, use symbols that occur to you (they need to make sense only to you) and different color pens or markers. Don't slow your brain down by trying to create art, but do use images, sketches, color-coding, and symbols liberally.

Once you write (in large print) your central topic in the middle of your map, you will branch the main ideas off this central image. Use one key word or symbol per line so your map stays neat and uncrowded enough to read easily. Your mind will automatically start to see how your words relate to each other. One key word copied from your idea collection page may give you an entirely new branch of related ideas on your map. Just keep going with it!

One author chose to start blogging as a precursor to writing her book. She considered the two main benefits as: 1) Getting into the practice and discipline of writing on a regular basis.   2) Discovering if she did in fact have a lot to say on a subject, and if it held her interest and that of readers. She calculated that after blogging for a good while, she would have a considerable amount of material already written to use in her book.

Asking herself, "What do I really want to blog about?" her answer revealed itself to her as she used the mind-mapping process. She was most strongly attracted to expanding on her ideas (based on her own background, expertise, and passion) about technology in education. As shown in the following illustration, her first three blogging topics, under her main topic of *Technology in Education*, are *Virtual Classroom, Electronic Textbooks,* and *Tech-Savvy Educators*. Note how these could later perfectly fit as chapter titles in her book..

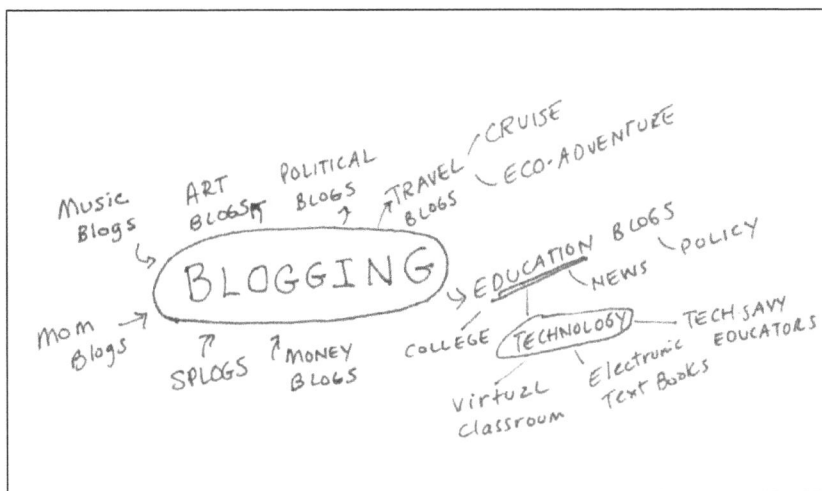

"Eureka! I will blog about everything 'tech' in the field of education!"

Mind-mapping is not mandatory, and it is not for everyone. But if you've used it before, you know how stimulating, exciting and fun this experience can be to people who are comfortable with it. When your whole brain is engaged and exercised like this, those *feel-good* chemicals are flowing and fueling you with even more motivation to move through this step. That is the reason mind-mapping, while not the only method of organizing your ideas, is certainly worth trying. Also, if you prefer technology and a screen to pen and paper whenever possible, there are mind-mapping software tools available. For example you can download a free version or upgrade to a professional version of this mind-mapping software at the web site of **xmind.net**.

Giving Form to Your Thoughts

You have already narrowed down the topics which you know and care about, and which topics are likely to interest your target readers. Then you collected, categorized and expanded your many thoughts on that subject. The next step is to ask yourself what is the best book content *format* to use to present this information. Without a format, you can waste a lot of time writing on your topic but never have it gel into an organized book someone would want to read.

There are many different organizational strategies to consider. Ask yourself which strategy is best suited to your content and purpose. Types of arrangements include sequential, chronological, order of importance, cause and effect, or compare/contrast. One smart approach is to start with a proven model. Here are a few examples of popular formats which are reader-oriented but also make your job of writing much easier.

A Brief Catalogue of Proven Format Models

As you search for what form your book should take, it is useful to consider some proven models. What follows are a few time-tested book formats that have proven track records in the marketplace. Adopting one makes good sense for an independent author. Instead of re-inventing the proverbial wheel, we advise you to take one of these established models and use it as a medium to hold your ideas, but of course customizing or enhancing it as you wish.

Nonfiction Book Format Examples

The # Of Ways to Do Something Book, or the How To __ Book

50 Simple Things You Can Do To Save the Earth by John Javna is a book that was originally self-published in 1990. It became a #1 bestseller, selling 5 million copies between 1990 and 1995, at which point it was taken out of print. An early success in the green movement, it inspired many books in the years after its publication.

The Avoiding Mistakes Book

People are always interested in learning from others' mistakes. A book which leaves the reader significantly more confident as they tackle something they must face is bound to be successful. *The Bell Lap: The 8 Biggest Mistakes To Avoid As You Approach Retirement* by Joseph Hearn is one of the millions of books with this format.

Ask The Guru Book

What is your special expertise? What questions are most commonly asked by people when they hear about what you do? As an information guru, you can create a FAQ (Frequently Asked Questions) book. People who identify with the topic love the idea of finding useful information all in one place – not only to answer the questions they have, but to answer questions they didn't think of but should have. Examples include *Questions and Answers: Contracts* by Keith A. Rowley, and *Is Yoga for Everyone? Professional Yoga Instructors and Studios Provide Real Answers to Real Questions!* by Tara Engeran, Edna Barr, William Cristobal and Mandy Lathan.

Collection Of Others' Wisdom Or Stories

Like the yoga book in the last example, one method to write a book is through group effort. This is especially true if you have access to people with extensive experience or great stories who are willing to share with you. A wealth of rich content can be organized into a highly attractive format. *Dear Jay, Love Dad: Bud Wilkenson's Letters to His Son* by Jay Wilkenson is a great example. Jay wrote the commentary and the background for each letter he shared from his famous (Oklahoma football and politics) father. Another example is the *"Chicken Soup"* series by Jack Canfield with over 112 million copies sold.

Memoirs Or Biography

Many people, especially the retired but not resigned, have undertaken the rewarding task of recording family stories, mainly for their grandchildren. To reach a broader audience, personal stories do not *have* to include famous people, but they do have to be compelling and offer value. Well-written memoirs and biographies can be found on every list of best-selling books. If your intention is to write a book which furthers *your* professional image, why is it sometimes a good idea to write a biography of someone else? Because readers are attracted to uniquely intriguing personal stories and cannot resist an opportunity to look behind the scenes. Just look for the connection to your own life's work so that you are attracting the very readers you want to introduce to your business.

For example, the owner of an antique store wrote a book about his grandfather who grew up Amish. The store owner's town was a tourist magnet for people curious about the area's Amish community and when they saw signs and flyers around town offering his book for free, they took time to find his antique store, come inside to get their free copy, and perhaps chat with the author. A large percentage of people who came in asking for the book also bought something – more than people who just came in to browse and hadn't come initially for the free book.

Timeless Words Book

Remember the article you were asked to write for the association magazine, or the twenty newsletter editions you published? Did you blog for a while or have a collection of blog material? You may have articles listed on your web site available for a free download. A doctor realized he already had an eBook nearly written when he remembered the nine different public seminars he had developed and presented. A business coach created three different eBooks from 900 success tips he wrote for his email contacts over the past several years.

How about Bronnie Ware? In Australia, this woman worked in people's homes caring for them in the last weeks of their lives. She wrote an article called *The Top Five Regrets of the Dying*. Because of the Internet, the article got around. After one year and over *one million* emails from people all over the world contacting her about the article, she decided to elaborate on the subject and published a book. It's a *top seller* on the Barnes & Noble website!

Look at anything you have previously written as potential material for a book. There is a golden opportunity to package your writing into a book or an eBook and publish a complete book in record time.

The Season Premiere Book

If you have followed these steps, you are already well on your way to writing and publishing your book. Keep your most compelling and motivating reasons clear and present by writing them down and keeping them in view. Refer to these when your energy lags or your writing isn't flowing as well as you hoped. Bouts of that are to be expected. Especially keep in mind the future picture of yourself on that day you are holding your finished book in your hand. You will want to leverage your accomplishment in many ways, one of which is to produce and release your *next* book! While you need to maintain a sharp focus on your first book project as you work on it, it is also helpful to know that once you've written one book, it is much easier to write the next one.

If you have processed and become comfortable with this chapter's keys to choosing your book topic and you can maintain focus as you work, ask yourself if it makes sense to break your book ideas up into multiple books or eBooks. If you have a subcategory of your topic which would end up being a very long chapter, it might make sense to have it stand on its own as the basis of a separate book. Each individual book launch is a perfect opportunity to gain public recognition, build your brand, announce exciting news to your growing audience, and capture more of your target market.

After Raleigh Pinskey wrote *101 Ways to Promote Yourself*, which was a huge hit, she analyzed her content and came up with several categories which she could build upon for additional eBooks. For example, she pulled out the information in her chapter about how to get name recognition, expanded it, and created *101 Ways to Get Name Recognition*.

Thinking ahead will make your series far easier to produce. When you are completing the processes in this chapter, you will find that some of your ideas can be categorized as starter material for a subsequent book or books. Once you've written your book, you can take the most compelling chapters and write new books or eBooks building on them. If you can parlay one book into three, you triple your profits and star power.

Consider the format examples offered in this chapter and choose one that both fits what you know and what inspires you. They are all tried-and-true formulas but if none of them seems to fit your book concept, then it's fine to create your own format. What's important is to begin to write and use the best structure of support to develop your ideas. Like all journeys, writing a book begins with a single *action* step.

You've Named The 'Who' And Developed The 'What' … Now For The 'How'

At this point, you know *who* you are writing for and *what* you want to communicate. You still have to figure out the *how*--the sequence. For example, your eBook may be a step-by-step guide. In that case, the obvious outline would be organized chronologically. In other instances, you must look at your main points, and sub-points, and put yourself in the readers' shoes to decide the best way to order your information.

For some authors, working through the decision-making process to narrow down and clarify their book topic is so intimidating they are stopped before really starting. Rather than worry about whether you've picked the perfect one, go with the result you achieved by working through this chapter.

"To dare is to lose one's footing momentarily. Not to dare is to lose oneself."

– Soren Kierkegaard

Keep in mind your goals and the day you will be holding your published book in hand. Some of the steps to your goals are highly creative; others are practical and linear. In the next chapter, you will be writing your outline, based on the work you accomplished in the processes just covered.

Key Distinctions For This Chapter

Idea Brainstorming vs. Mind-Mapping   A precursor to using mind-mapping as a tool to gain clarity and get your book started is to brainstorm ideas in a more free flow process. You are an experienced, educated person with valuable ideas and insights, and you have more than enough in your mind's memory files to write your book. By using idea brainstorming, you call out those many ideas from your mind and note them on paper. The results are general, not yet specific. Later, since your target audience does not want or need *most* of what is stored in your brain – only the particular information which is going to help them with their specific challenges and questions – you must narrow down the ideas. You can use mind-mapping to help focus, simplify, and organize these ideas.

First Book Project vs. Subsequent Book(s) It is estimated that a second book project (of similar scope and length as one's first publication) will require about 40% less time and effort. As you work through the many steps to clarify your ideas, give purpose and form to your book, and see it through to publication, keep in mind the probability you will be able to capitalize on your learning curve for future successes. As you gather your existing intellectual property from past articles, speeches or blogs you've written, you may find enough material, or distinct topics, to write more than one book. In fact, a book which is designated "first of a series" is usually more attractive to a target reader or book agent. Know that the first book project you complete can provide momentum and confidence to leverage even more of your expertise and creativity.

Summary

With your wealth of knowledge and experience, the challenge is not coming up with a good idea for a book. Your job is to choose the ideal book topic for *this* book, giving consideration to what excites you as well as your target audience. Your topic, once chosen, can ignite your mind to pop like popcorn with ideas. You must creatively capture the multitude of ideas in your mind and then narrow them down to ideally fit this particular book project.

Then, you must further simplify, categorize and visually organize your topic contents. Mind-mapping is an excellent tool for this step. You will have a much better grasp of your whole book concept after that, and then you can analyze the best approach to use as a format. You may use a proven one such as "50 Ways to Instantly Improve Your _____" or come up with your own design.

As you develop your book idea, don't be surprised if you start to see a second book forming in your mind. Decide what you want to include in *this* book, and organize the materials and ideas into categories which may end up being your chapters. Notice if you are getting bogged down in this decision-making step and letting fear or perfectionism stop you. Go with the process flow and keep your end goals in mind. Now you are ready to start drawing the blueprint in earnest – you are ready to write your book outline.

Chapter VI

An Outline For Book/EBook Success

**Every Book Needs A Great Outline—
Here's How To Create Yours**

An Outline For Book and eBook Success

Just as most builders would not put up a building without an architectural drawing and most drivers check a map to go someplace unfamiliar, you, as an author, need a good outline for your book or eBook. The use of an outline to write your book is analogous to a builder using blueprints or architectural drawings to construct a house. Even if you are not writing the book, and you choose to have a professional writer do most or all of your book for you, think how much better they can produce what you want if you've created the outline for them to follow.

Outlining is the process of focusing, organizing, and creating a blueprint or roadmap for writing a book from beginning to end. Good writing almost always starts with such a plan. Creating and using an outline will make your life as an author markedly easier. While creating an outline takes time and focused thinking initially, the actual writing process becomes much easier and faster when you have done so — and using an outline results in a better book.

Your outline will serve as your road map as it will depict a specific route to take to get from point to point, and will be very helpful during your project in determining how far you have progressed and how far you have to go.

Even if you are not sure how to use outlining effectively, the concept is probably familiar to you. In the process of organizing just about anything, you start with the main subject and create categories within that subject so that objects or ideas which are alike can be found more easily. Within a category there may be one or more subcategories.

We have learned to expect information to be delivered in a well-organized form just as we expect everyday processes to be organized in familiar ways. If, for example, you bring home a new spoon, you first go to the kitchen, then to the silverware drawer, then to the utensil divider, then to the spoon slot, so that it is placed where it can easily be found by anyone familiar with a typical household layout, i.e., an organization scheme which makes sense at a glance. Just as you would assume that you could find a spoon in a neighbor's house because of learned expectations, book readers have expectations about how content is organized which you must consider.

The last thing you want to do is to confuse and frustrate your reader. When you write your book using a well-planned outline, you will please yourself and your reader.

Advantages Of An Outline

No matter what kind of outline you use, using an outline has some big advantages.

- An outline provides you with a birds-eye view of your project so you can see how your ideas flow.

- It gives you the opportunity to test alternative idea flows, to move things around and see if one flow works better than others before you write and have to move entire sections around and write new transitions between sections. Note that this is best done in consultation with your editor or publishing partner.

- By following an outline, you can pick up your writing at any time and know where you are, and where you need to go at that moment.

- Using an outline allows you to more easily share ideas with editors and co-authors.

- An outline hastens the day you will finish your book and feel confident that it is ready to publish. When you have your outline in front of you, it's easy to isolate sections to work on, so the book actually gets done. Because you aren't facing the task of writing your whole book at once, it makes the whole process much more manageable.

Defining The Book Outline

An outline is a formal document that you create as you decide which ideas will go into your book. It organizes your thoughts and provides the skeletal structure of your book. It delineates the parts of your book in a hierarchical structure that progresses from one section to another, usually employing an alternating series of numbers and letters, indented accordingly, to indicate levels of importance. It is essential to the nonfiction writing process.

Many unfinished books sit in a drawer somewhere, frustrating the author who ultimately abandons them because they suffer from a fundamental structural problem. It is very difficult to write something as lengthy as a book without an outline. Such a blueprint represents a plan which is at least two steps beyond just having a good idea for a book.

An eBook outline can benefit from a fair degree of detail compared to an outline for a traditional book intended for print because the market expectations of an eBook are different from printed books. Here are some guidelines that will help you to adapt your outlining technique to the unique characteristics of the eBook format.

- Since the marketplace has created expectations among eBook readers that an eBook length is shorter than a print book on the same topic, every word within them counts and should be carefully chosen. Thus, a fairly detailed, carefully researched, and well-organized outline helps your eBook manuscript stay focused. Using our road map analogy, if you start to ramble or get off-topic, it is like taking a wrong turn which referring to your outline will help you correct quickly.

- Because your outline provides a birds-eye view of your entire project and how ideas and messages flow from one section to the next, it is the ideal place to put "markers" or "placeholders" for your planned illustrations and dynamic elements/multimedia components that amplify the message contained in the text. We usually put our dynamic element placeholders in red text so we don't confuse them with another outline item. The instructional phrase will be deleted before publishing.

Outline Techniques

Creating a good outline is not a haphazard process of listing ideas on a page and trying to organize them later, hoping a coherent book emerges. First, it requires you to think about your target readers and what they are likely to expect to find in a book on your topic. Also, creating an effective outline requires you to organize your thoughts and explore the key concepts you will want to include in your book before you begin outlining. As explained previously in the chapter on choosing your topic, tapping into all your ideas on your topic, and then using a mind-map to clarify and organize them, are excellent steps to take before trying to tackle an outline.

A book's professional quality, whether digital or print, will be a reflection of the outline which supports it, whether that outline is formally written like a blueprint or created loosely like a sketch. Don't try to keep it only in your head – write it out so you don't have to depend on your mental powers of organization and recall to keep your writing on track. You won't be writing your entire book at one sitting, so having your outline handy will enable you to stop and start more easily.

How To Write Your Outline

You may have learned a "correct" or preferred formula or technique for setting up an outline in school or on the job. If you are comfortable with the outlining technique that you learned, by all means use it to outline your book. If you need a formulaic and time-tested method for outlining an book, you can use the example at the end of this chapter or a variation based on it. This particular outline example will enable you to write a book in a very streamlined manner, and could help you write and finish your first draft in a matter of days if that is your goal.

Use Tools You Know

For outlining, most writers use a computer with word processing software. Some writers, who are more numerically-inclined, use a spreadsheet to take advantage of its ability to sort and rearrange cells that contain ideas. Others, especially those who like mind-mapping, even use a pencil or marker to create their outline before they transfer it to a computer file.

They all work. Our advice is to use what you are comfortable with, know, and like. Then use whatever format you come up with consistently. As long as it continues to produce good results for you, you'll be on the right track. Spend your precious time researching and organizing your ideas instead of learning new software or outlining techniques.

Choose A Style

There are many styles of outlines. A common one is the Formal Outline style. It uses Roman Numerals, letters and numbers. It usually starts with your book's *Table of Contents*, then proceeds to main headings with Roman Numerals, and sub-headings under each main heading using letters. It then proceeds to finer and finer subheadings and topics, alternating numbers and letters. Note that headings should not be full, polished sentences but can be phrases or sentence fragments. What's important is to use key words. Since you are the user of the outline, you should be very clear about headings, subheadings and, if you find them useful, sub-sub headings.

Formal? Casual? Use An Outline Style That Fits You

Choose a level of detail that works for you. It's your book and it contains your ideas, so make your outline as detailed or loose as you want it to be as long as it works as a reliable and consistent blueprint for your writing, and acts as a catalyst for you to fully express your ideas.

Automatic outlining conventions that are built into mainstream word processing software are formal and limited and may not suit your style. You can turn off the automatic outlining format in Microsoft Word® or other word processors and build your outline yourself. Don't be afraid to move things, cross them out, and whatever it takes until you are comfortable that your blueprint/outline will work as a helpful guide as you write your book. Remember that even though your outline can resemble a *Table of Contents*, it is only for you, the author, to utilize, so feel free to self-style it to meet your needs.

The exception is if you plan to write an outline to submit with a proposal to a book agent or publishing houses. You will need to work on a more formalized version than you personally need since they respond more favorably to the clarity of a formal style. Also, if you are writing a multi-author book, a formal outline technique is recommended because of its clarity. This clarity provides a good framework for each co-author to understand the whole book, what the other author(s) are doing, and how and where to best make his or her contributions to the manuscript.

Many times you have illustrations, photographs, or diagrams in mind which will be incorporated into your manuscript. Go ahead and note these and their placement on your outline. If you are planning an eBook that has multimedia embedded, make sure that you include in your outline your specification of what particular element is to be placed in which section.

The Book/Ebook Express: A Three-Step Method From Outline To Finish Line

Using this particular formula, you can start and finish a complete first draft of your book in as little as a few days. With this format, you will end up with a manuscript of approximately 100 pages. When you have invested your time carefully, chosen your topic as discussed in Chapter II, honed in on your title, general purpose and content, you are ready to make use of this format as one way to write your book.

You have three main tasks which you should be able to complete by referring to your mind-map or other content organization notes.

> 1.   Title (as created with SEO process in a previous chapter.)
>
> 2.   Chapter Headings: Use your chosen outline format and title each of six chapters.
>
> 3.   Under each Chapter, 4-8 points that reflect key points/benefits of that chapter.

Example: Author Outline Produced With The Ebook Express Method

In the example that follows, the author created the outline by referring to her organized and categorized notes which were diagrammed using a format similar to a mindmap, a Venn

Diagram. In Chapter II in this book there is an example which you can refer to for the creative details and an illustration of this complete and color-coded diagram.

From her diagram notes, the author started an outline and filled in the blanks, i.e. followed it by using the aforementioned three-step process to create the outline below. Note the chapter headings and sub-headings at this stage are written for the purpose of guiding the author through the entire process of writing her eBook. Later, these headings will be edited and converted into strong Search Engine Optimized (SEO-compatible) chapter titles.

(Beginning of Outline)

**The Speaker's Mirror: How To See, Hear
And Deliver What Your Audience Craves**

Introduction

Chapter I   Establish Connection with Non-Verbal Communication

    1. Face talk
    2. Gestures and body talk
    3. Tone and energy of voice and breath
    4. Matching movement with message

Chapter II   Four Keys to Perfecting Content

    1. Strong opening and closing
    2. Organizing and supporting your points
    3. Use of Story
    4. Demonstrate mastery of subject

Chapter III   How an Audience-Centered Speech Excites Them and Calms You

    1. Use a topic your audience can relate to, or give yours that angle
    2. Invite interaction
    3. Use of Story
    4. Knowledge of topic used to demonstrate, not dominate

Chapter IV   Authenticity: Be Known as the Real Deal
    1. How non-verbal and verbal presentation affects authenticity
    2. How to clarify your purpose and message
    3. Using personal stories to build trust
    4. Sit in your own audience

Chapter V   Enthusiasm! Rouse Your Audience
    1. Why enthusiasm is crucial to speaking success
    2. How to get un-bored and re-energize yourself with your topic
    3. Draw out audience head nods, laughs, answers out loud, and applause
    4. Empower vs. motivate so audience is more deeply enthused or inspired to action

Chapter VI   Respect: It's a Mutual Thing
    1. Setting the stage for mutual respect
    2. The quickest way to lose your audience
    3. How to keep your content respectfully audience-centered
    4. Not too long, not too short – how to get it just right

Summary

(End of Outline)

Writing Your Book From Your Outline

At this juncture, you have reached another milestone in your path to publishing success. Now you are facing the blank first page of your book. Take a deep breath and proceed. You are an author and you are about to begin the first complete draft of your book.

You have an outline, your blueprint, to guide you along the way. You are ready to assemble your helpful resources (found in the next chapter) and utilize the writing process tips throughout this book.

Key Distinctions For This Chapter

Outline vs. Mind Map   Mind-mapping generates ideas and thought trails, and organizes random ideas into categories. It is not a blueprint or ordered list of contents, whereas an outline is that kind of structured guide.

Outlining vs. Writing   Outlining creates chapters and sub-chapters to break up the content to make it reader-friendly, and to provide the author a roadmap to follow during the writing process. The outline is not created for the reader to see – it's a tool for the author. The writing process uses language and sentences to develop and present each point under each chapter heading. Writing from an outline is helpful for the author, and results in better content for the reader.

Summary

As you begin, keep in mind that outlines come in many forms. There is no one perfect or universal outline form. Many different techniques will work. It is important to choose a technique that will work for you. Be advised that the outline is an essential writing tool. Skipping the outlining step in an attempt to save time will result in spending extra time and can cause frustration during the writing process. With your outline, you are well on your way to building your book by following your blueprint. It makes the writing process simpler, better, and less time-consuming.

Chapter VII

Assemble Your Resources

Tools, Technology And Your Checklist For Self-Publishing Success

Assemble Your Writing and Technology Resources

Writing a book is a major undertaking whether the book is going to be published as an eBook (digital formats) or if it will be printed. Just as with any large and complex project, getting the job done with efficiency, focus, and in a timely fashion is made much easier by having the right tools at your disposal. Just as it is possible to build a house with a hammer and handsaw, experienced builders would not think of starting without their proper power tools.

Checklist of Writing Resources For True Self-Publishers

Fortunately, while writing a good nonfiction book requires knowledge of the language, a good idea for a topic, and knowledge of the subject, it does not absolutely require a lot of high tech or expensive equipment. You can do it with a pen, pencil, and a pad or notebook, and then pay somebody to take your manuscript and type (word process) it so you can submit it to a printer or eBook publisher. Most of us choose another route, though.

To the extent that you are working with a publisher who can supply some of the resources listed in this checklist (such as editing, proofreading, eBook formatting and conversion software and marketing services,) you will not need each and every one of them. Nevertheless, most of them come in very handy for any writer and will make a huge difference between writing as inefficient and difficult work versus writing as a pleasant, efficient, and satisfying process.

If you are going to truly self-publish without assistance, you will need to assemble and master all of these resources and processes. Unless you have a great deal of time and interest, and are probably going to self-publish more than one book, you would be wise to learn about these resources while keeping in mind which of these you want to outsource. Included here are what is needed for both digital and print versions.

We suggest that you copy this checklist and check things off as you assemble them. Then, before your begin to write, make certain that you familiarize yourself about each resource or process. Then you can decide what tasks to tackle yourself and what to delegate.

Non Computer Technology

☐ **Barnes & Noble account** to upload your book for sale as a Nook eBook.

☐ **Amazon Kindle account** to upload your book for sale as a Kindle book.

☐ **Apple iTunes account and/or Apple iBooks account**. Note that Apple states that "if you submit your work for publication in the in the iBookstore as an iBook file (and) if a fee is charged for the work …in the iBook format, the work may only be sold through the iBookstore." If the work is in a different format, such as PDF or epub, this restriction does not apply. You may distribute the work on your own website if the work is provided free of charge or sold in a format other than the iBook format (such as PDF or epub). If you wish to sell your work in the iBook format, it may only be sold through the iBookstore. Note that this is true in mid-2013, but may change as Apple deals with the U.S. Justice Department anti-trust proceedings against the company, and as the industry evolves.

☐ **A writer's space.** Environment matters. You, and your writing, will be affected by your surroundings. Writing can be inspiring, but sometimes solitary and tiring, so you should find a pleasant place to work and not only equip it with the resources you need as a writer, but also make it a pleasant sanctuary with "comfort" décor. Contrary to legend, most writers don't work in a café.

☐ **Good furniture and lighting**. At a minimum, you'll need a comfortable, ergonomically acceptable chair and a desk with enough space for your computer and your other writing tools. Eyestrain can also be a problem for writers so make sure that your writing space has even and ample lighting. Pay attention to the room layout too. Having a window to view a distant scene occasionally helps avoid eye strain.

☐ **Quiet space**. If you are like most of us, you'll find that it is hard to write well in the middle of chaos or distractions from family or co-workers. Try to locate your writing place (whether it is your private office with a door you can close, or shared space) in a quiet zone. Many times it is not the place, it's the time of day which allows for quiet, focused time. So use your calendar as a tool to block out early morning or other times you have the best chance of quiet, uninterrupted work.

☐ **A network** of encouraging and supportive friends, relatives and supporters, in-person or online, helps immensely to give you positive strokes for what you are doing and provide people to discuss your ideas and progress. In most cases, you do not want to have a spouse, parent or best friend giving editorial advice, just encouragement. If you find it useful, a writing buddy can be a good resource to hold you accountable for your writing progress. Set up a structure via email and/or phone.

☐ **Motivation.** Make a contract with yourself to commit to writing your book, and to overcome obstacles which come up. Identify your personal and compelling reasons to write your book, and your goals for your book, and write them down to keep you motivated. When you are truly motivated, you'll find a way to make it happen.

☐ **Mission statement for your work.** Knowing why you are writing your current book and what you want to accomplish with it is a big advantage for maintaining focus and keeping your work on track. Some writers print it, frame it and put it on the wall in their writing space.

☐ **Target reader definition**. If you have the people that you want to read your book in mind as you write, your book will be more likely to respond to their wants and needs. Email surveys are one simple, free method to conduct your own market research.

☐ **Timeline.** As an important clause in your contract with yourself, commit to spending time on your writing every single day, even if it is just enough time to write a paragraph or two. It is also very important to set a date to finish your book. Be realistic. It probably won't be done in a month (unless you have huge blocks of time and motivation,) but there is no reason it has to take years either. Your creativity can best flourish when you have a structure, a finish date goal, and daily writing habit.

☐ **Dictionary.** A good dictionary (either online or printed) is helpful to check spelling, look up meanings, and even help with synonyms, although a thesaurus is preferable for the latter. During your first draft you shouldn't stop and spend time perfecting your wording or spelling, but when you are editing and proofing, do not rely solely on your software spelling-checker – it does not replace your need for a dictionary.

☐ **Thesaurus. A** thesaurus is a good tool to search for synonyms and the right substitute word so you don't repeat the same term too much. Merriam Webster's dot.com site and dictionary.com both offer, for free, a useful dictionary and a thesaurus.

☐ **Grammar assistance.** While we do not recommend that writers rely on the grammar suggestions built in to typical word processors, if you need grammar guidance a good place to seek it is online at grammar sites dedicated to providing quick answers to FAQs.

☐ **Style guide.** Using and maintaining a sensible style is important for writers. Consult a good style guide. One good example is the Associated Press (AP) Stylebook which you can find by visiting that web site.

☐ **Writers' journals, magazines, ezines and web sites** are very helpful sources of tips, techniques and inspiration. You can sign up for the free **Suncoast Digital Press Author Tips & Techniques** at the Suncoast Digital Press web site.

☐ **Books**. You are a writer. Writers read. There are great books by veteran writers, no matter what type of book you are developing – learn from those who have gone through the process before. One excellent example is *On Writing: A Memoir of the Craft* by Stephen King. Another type of book it's good to have handy is a book of quotations such as *Bartlett's.*

☐ **A lawyer.** Writing and publishing (especially independent publishing) require knowledge about copyright procedures, intellectual property, fair use, and other legal issues. We recommend consulting a qualified lawyer for current and accurate information.

☐ **Specialized reference documents** in your field are indispensable to look up arcane or technical terms.

☐ **ISBN procedure knowledge, ISBN forms and a place to file them** are required to give your book or eBook an International Standard Book Number. Note that the convention is to obtain a separate ISBN for digital and print editions. An accompanying bar code is recommended for both. Some booksellers require bar codes to include price.

☐ **An editor.** Every writer needs a human editor. No matter how adept you might be at editing the work of others, it is extremely difficult to edit your own work since we tend to not "see" our own errors, disorganization, lack of clarity, or omissions.

☐ **A proofreader.** As with editing, no matter how competent you might be at proofreading the work of others, you need somebody other than yourself to proofread your manuscript. Errors do happen. (Proofing software helps but is not a 100% reliable substitute for a good human proofer.)

☐ **A digital audio recorder** will allow you to save your thoughts about your book as you drive or are otherwise not in a place you can write down your ideas.

☐ **Video equipment and setting.** A high-quality video camera (either built into a digital SLR camera, a top-of-the-line smart phone or tablet, or a video-only camera) is very useful to shoot raw footage for the dynamic elements you may want to include in your dynamic eBook. You will need a sturdy tripod too.

You also should have a suitable video-taping setting with good lighting, and an uncluttered and quiet background. It is not essential to have a full studio, professional backdrops, or a green screen – you can even shoot in your office or outside in a quiet place.

Video editing software is a good thing to have too, although unless you have the skills to use this often-complex software, you might be better off having a videographer or an outside service to edit your raw video clips. It is very desirable to have professional-looking dynamic elements to embed in your eBook, or a video trailer for your author web site and other promotional opportunities. To see one short video which serves as both a book trailer for marketing purposes, and as a dynamic element inside the author's eBook, please use your smartphone free App for this QR code we have embedded for your convenience. (In the eBook version of this book, this is a hyperlink dynamic element.)

Computer Technology

Computers are a writer's best friend. Used correctly, they can be a tireless administrative assistant and allow you to do more in less time. Nevertheless, you are well advised to keep the computer programmer's saw "garbage in-garbage out" in mind. The trick is to use your tools instead of letting them use you. Use computer technology when it can help you accomplish your goals and make you quicker, better organized, and more efficient. But don't try to make your tools do what they are not designed to accomplish, or you'll fail to get the job done and be frustrated in the process.

☐ **A computer.** While your computer does not have to be the latest and greatest, it should have enough power to operate reliably while you write, and to run software like a good word processor and perhaps a drawing or illustration program, and a few others that are detailed below.

It can be a laptop or a desktop, but it needs a comfortable keyboard, sufficient storage capacity for your all of your book projects with their supporting research, video or photo files, documents, and the ability to run useful software such as a word processor and a browser. Tablet computers are very convenient, but unless they have the ability to use a full-sized keyboard as an attachment, they are limited as a writer's tool. And, by the way, a superb book can be written using either a PC or a Mac.

☐ **A USB flash memory drive** to hold each book project you are working on. This small data storage device, also called a "thumb drive," is removable and rewritable. It can be used to store a copy of your book-related files for safe-keeping or mobility. Devices with 8 GB (gigabytes) are very economical and considered adequate in most cases. (Learn how to utilize these devices as part of your book marketing in Chapter XI.)

☐ **Word processors** are very useful for writing and proofreading. (They are not capable of professional-level graphic design work.)

☐ **Internet Access** for research and marketing. (You can also outsource research affordably.)

☐ **Browsers** Up-to-date web browsing software (preferably more than one brand) is essential to research and market your book. Some have useful special features, for example "Google Images" can help you find illustrations, photos or graphics to enhance your book. The more familiar you are with how browsers work, the more you will understand how prospective readers can discover your book while searching the Internet.

☐ **A web domain** for your author web site and access to a web designer or web design software if you are designing you own site. (As soon as you have your book's title finalized, register it so you own the domain name.) Options to consider are: a web site exclusively for your book(s); a site primarily about you which includes info about books you've authored; adding content about your book(s) to an existing site, such as your business site. It still makes sense to own the domain name for your book and direct its web traffic to the site you choose.

☐ **Drawing programs** come in handy to create or edit illustrations.

☐ **Photo-editing programs** to crop and otherwise manipulate photographs for your book.

☐ **Adobe Acrobat** (not Adobe Acrobat Reader) or other software to create/edit PDF files.

☐ **Conversion software** programs that can take either a PDF or Word® file input and output a mobi, epub and other needed file outputs. Sigil, Jutoh and Calibre are some of current crop. Note that the learning curve is steep and the output is often restricted to certain formats in the current iterations of most of this software. (Booksellers such as Amazon and Barnes & Noble require these special formats, so if you want your eBook offered there, your manuscript must undergo conversion.)

☐ **Social media accounts** for Twitter, LinkedIn, and Facebook, at a minimum. Pinterest and Google+ are also recommended. With research, you can often find social media specific to your particular niche which has fewer, but more targeted, members. You also need a system for consistent engagement (updates, posts, comments, etc.) to have social media be of any use in your book marketing strategy.

☐ **A spreadsheet** for tracking expenses, royalties, submissions and marketing results. Microsoft Excel® is standard and more than adequate.

☐ **Proofreading software** is helpful, though not a complete substitute for what a good proofreader can catch. Two examples are PerfectIt and WhiteSmoke.

Key Distinction For This Chapter

Self-Directed Publishing vs. Doing Everything Yourself
"Self" publishing does not mean you are all on your own. Learn the steps and understand the process but be honest about your own

strengths, interests, and personal time and energy available – use resources and outside experts when it makes sense. Failing to outsource can lead to failure to finish and publish your book.

Summary

"Publishing" is a term used to describe the process of getting a completed manuscript properly formatted, printed (either digitally or standard) and to market. "Self-Publishing" is a term used to differentiate between the old model (the traditional publishing house being in charge of this process) vs. you the author maintaining control of many key decisions and especially the timeline. Also sometimes this is called "independent" or "indie" publishing.

Now that you have at least a basic idea of the kind of resources you will need as an author and independent publisher, you are in a good position to make an informed decision whether to truly self-publish without any professional help, or to seek assistance on certain steps of your project based on your review of this checklist.

While the checklist is to be taken seriously, we do not recommend delaying the start of writing your book only because you do not yet have all the recommended tools and resources at hand. As one client so eloquently put it, "Don't spend all day saddling up!"

Chapter VIII

Cover Design

Capture Your Audience With A Great Book Cover

A Cover Can Crush Your Success Or Send You Soaring

As an author or professional writing a book that you will self-publish for business purposes, you already know what a book can do for you:

- Establish your credibility as an expert.
- Be a strong magnet to attract your target audience to your web site.
- Position you as an authority in your field – the go-to person for your peers and clients and even the media.
- Set you apart with an instantly recognizable brand.
- Create a passive stream of income as your book sales soar on Amazon and other book sales sites.
- Be your foundation or keystone product to build into multiple profit-building products.
- Win the attention of publishers and distributors or book reviewers.
- Consistently receive more and higher-paying speaking and consulting opportunities.

An excellent book cover is not simply a nice finishing touch or a marketing tool for your book; it is crucial to achieving the benefits listed above, and to giving you the best results whatever your personal goals are for your book.

You *Will* Be Judged By Your Cover So Take Advantage Of It

A book is not like any other product when it comes to a buyer's decision-making process. As much as 75% of the choice is based on the *cover*, according to top booksellers like Barnes & Noble. The marketability of a book is determined not only by its content and the qualifications or fame of the author, but also by the design, packaging and price of the book or eBook.

It's an old saying that you can't judge a book by its cover, but this maxim does not hold true in the real world of commercial bookselling. People *do* judge a book by its cover – not only readers but also major decision makers like chain store buyers, wholesale buyers, and even television and movie producers. They can make a world-changing decision about a book in a few seconds, and all they've done is look at the title, cover, and sized up the packaging. That's it.

Actor and director Sean Penn in a past issue of *Entertainment Weekly* was asked about when he decided to make Jon Krakauer's *Into the Wild* into a film. "When the book first came out, I wandered into a bookstore, saw it on the shelf, judged the book by its cover, took it home, read it twice, finally fell asleep, woke up and started trying to see if the rights were available. I had a very strong feeling that this thing was dying to get out of the pages and onto the screen."

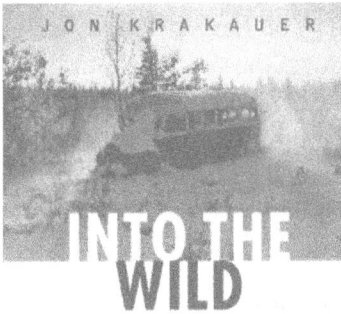

Penn also talked about the book cover *Into the Wild* in a recent interview in *Time* magazine: "The cover grabbed me – the bus, the image of the bus with the title *Into the Wild* on it…"

That's how a cover should work. It should draw potential readers to the book, and get them to pick it up and read it. The cover is not only a keystone to the initial impression, but also for the potential of follow-up sales, including movie rights and other subsidiary rights.

Choosing Your Ideal Cover Elements: What Is Your Category Or Book Type?

Your book cover must look appropriate to the subject. For example, we have come to expect that business books should, and do, have a different look than fiction, poetry, or history books. Readers expect *Windows for Dummies* to have one particular look, and romance novels to portray quite a different image. From across a room you could tell the difference between *Harry Potter* and *Roget's Thesaurus*.

What category best describes your book? Check online booksellers and also visit bookstores and notice the common design approach used by the books in your category. You want to fit into that category so people recognize your book's genre and will feel comfortable with its look. With the right cover style, they will know enough about what to expect from your book that they will be induced to look at it. Of course, you want your book to stand out too, but first it must be accepted and understood within the right context. For professionals, your brand informs your book cover, and your book cover influences your brand.

Can You Read And Understand The Title's Words In Less Than Three Seconds?

Make sure your title is easy to read. You have just a few seconds to make a good impression, inform the reader about the topic, entice them with what's in it for them, and persuade them to choose your book from a vast number of options. As discussed in Chapter IV, when developing your title, a *short* title is best for many reasons, one of which is the words can be large and still fit on your book cover. Readability is paramount. If your cover was on a standard, printed 6" x 9" book, could you read it from across the room? Bold type is generally best. Avoid all capitals unless your title is five words or less, and don't get fancy with the font. 𝔒𝔩𝔡 𝔈𝔫𝔤𝔩𝔦𝔰𝔥 may match your theme but is not easy to read at a glance.

Also, contrast is very important. Put light-colored type over a dark background, or dark type over a light background. A small, black drop shadow behind the title is one design element sometimes used to help visibility. As in any good graphic design, keep it clean and simple.

Your subtitle will contain more words and should be in a smaller font. You might use a different typeface for the subtitle because that would add interest to the cover while making a clear distinction between the different messages. Good combinations are: sans serif and serif, roman and italic, capitals and lower case, bold and thin.

What Colors Communicate Your Brand And Appeal To Your Ideal Target Reader?

Because color communicates feeling and its many nuances, use it with care. Don't go crazy with colors just to get attention. Children's books may be the exception, which helps us remember that a tax attorney's book should not look like a bedtime storybook. Contrast works effectively, but harmony also works well. Opposite (complementary) colors are great, but limit the use of that effect to only once on the cover. After that, apply harmonizing, less contrasting colors, such as pale against darker intense shades of the same color. Some general points: red is hot, gets attention; blue is less visible, but evokes solidity and authority; yellow is optimistic; green is healthy, food, leisure; brown is rich, traditional, warm; white is pure, credible; black is sensuous, mysterious or authoritative.

Should You Use A Full Spectrum Of Colors Or A High Contrast Two-Color Cover?

If you are planning to use a traditional printing company to print covers for bound books, you will find that a "four-color process" cover is more expensive than a two-color or black and white cover. One of the huge advantages to publishing an eBook is there is no printing cost at all, no matter how many colors you use. However, you will probably be printing promotional materials featuring your book cover such as a flyer about a workshop you are offering, or a business card created for your book and its web site. Two-color covers can be done successfully, but their design must be strong to overcome the limitations. Our advice is to go with a full-color cover especially if you can use a photograph as an attractive graphic element. The added impact and visual attraction benefit is usually worth the extra printing cost.

Be aware that some marketing materials and general publicity will likely show your book cover in black and white, so make a reduced photocopy of the cover to see how well it reads and whether its impact means that those who view it will know what your book is about in three seconds. It is possible to create a cover that works well in either color or black and white if you are mindful of that during the design process.

Can Your Cover Stand On Its Own?

A book cover is a valuable piece of real estate. People will make a decision about your book in a matter of seconds and in some cases from a tiny two-centimeter size image on their smart phone. The cover is what introduces a book to a customer, to its intended reader. For eBooks, the cover must entice the browsing reader to stop and find out more by reading a description, or peak "inside" to the *Table of Contents* or other interior page, or read a book review. For a printed and bound book, the cover must inspire the handler to open the book or at least turn to the back cover to read descriptive sales copy. Like a handshake, your cover can provide a great introduction or a weak first impression.

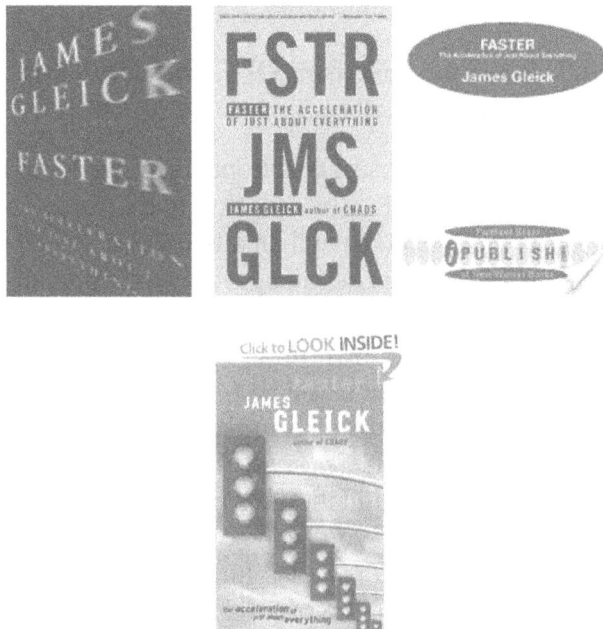

In the images above, James Gleick's book *Faster* is shown with four very different looks. Different covers are sometimes used to attract different reader profiles, or to update the look of the book to appeal to those who are looking for current releases. A revised version or newly enhanced version (e.g. a dynamic eBook version) may warrant a new cover.

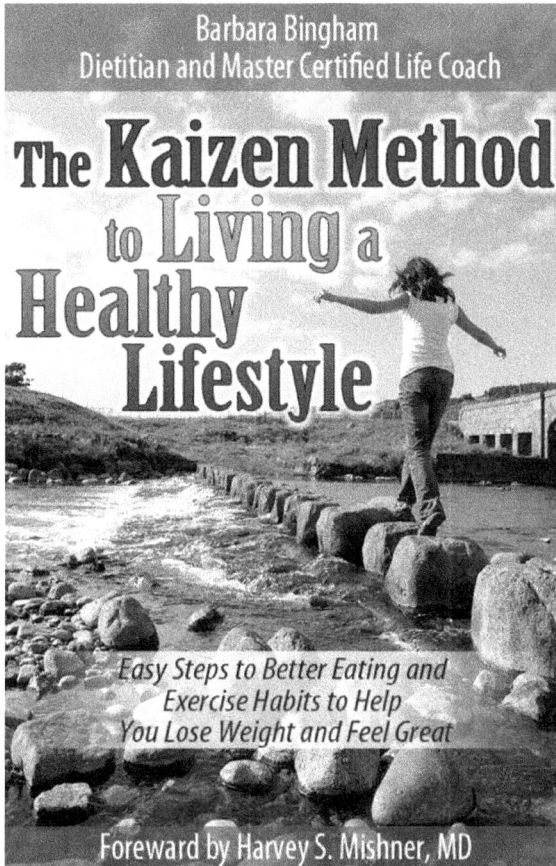

Why Do We Like The Cover For *The Kaizen Method* EBook?

- Title is in large easy-to-read typeface.
- Title stands out against contrasting, lighter background.
- Subtitle is different, contrasting, smaller font (and has SEO key words.)
- Full color allows use of attractive and fitting photograph.

- Green, blue and grey communicate health plus content with substance.

- Photo perfectly communicates feeling of joy and fresh, healthy energy.

- Photo indicates book will show easy-to-follow "steps."

- Even though it is not a traditionally printed book cover, it looks like it.

- Author and credentials are visible but don't compete with title or image.

- The image is tailored to the target audience (women.)

- The author's credibility is enhanced by the Foreword author's M.D. title.

Yes! You Need A BACK Cover For Your eBook

It is true that an eBook's "cover" is simply a computer-generated graphic image. Nonetheless, it needs to look like it represents a printed-on-heavy-paper book cover. This applies to both "front" and "back" eBook covers. For thousands of years, books have had a front and back cover, so it is important to meet reader expectations even when your book is only digital and doesn't really have a physical front or back. Your finalized book file, ready to upload to online bookstores, should have the front cover as the first page and the back cover as the last page. This one step goes a long way to satisfy readers that they are seeing a "book" on their tablet, e-reader, computer, or smart phone.

Whether on a printed promotional piece or on your web site, you can feature both the front and back covers of your eBook. That gives you a significant marketing advantage if your back cover is well designed. Most back covers include endorsements which may not be easily viewed elsewhere. Also, many eBook authors decide to secure a small quantity of printed and bound books published through a POD (Print On Demand) service. When you are speaking to a group or setting up any type of display it is useful to have at least one physical book people can see. So, of course both a front and back cover will be needed for a printed version.

What Goes On A Back Cover?

Reach for a couple of books right now from your bookshelf and look at the back covers. A superbly written heading or description can really help sell the book. It should beckon the reader, tempting him with choice tidbits and making him hungry for what's being served up inside. It should be provocative and engaging enough to hook a potential reader's interest, yet not give away so much of the contents so that the bait is gobbled up in just one bite and your reader is not "hooked."

It is a mistake to waste space repeating the book title at the top of the back cover. Since the reader already saw the title on the front and was interested enough to look at the back, it is better to use that valuable space to "wow" them with a provocative question or headline that highlights the #1 benefit of your book or a unique selling point of your book.

The following example of the back cover of Brock Lee's *The General Mangler* shows see how this valuable real estate is used to pique and drive the readers' interest.

On the back cover of Meaningful Sounds, note the book title is not repeated as the header. A more intriguing headline draws the reader in. Also, the prominent use of endorsements to tell about the book is more effective than a long written description.

STEP INTO THE LIFE OF WWII VETERAN NATHAN POLSKY

Through rhyme, humor and insights, his poetry will warm your heart with a sentimental story or light-hearted witty wisdom.

I love the whimsical and fun-loving nature of Polsky's verse...in the spirit of Lewis Carroll and Ogden Nash. If you don't believe me, read "Backwards, March!" (Hello, I must be going now...Goodbye I'll stay awhile....Why don't you sit and also stand...An inch is still a mile.) or "Awesome"(My voice was fantastic! A triumph of tone...with such dazzling vocal power...spectacular, thrilling, until I hurt myself...taking bows in the shower.).

--Jim Reed, editor, Birmingham Arts Journal

Readers who will enjoy this book most are those who share the time-frame involved and the poet's view of life. Very few poems are subtle, but many are humorous and possess a clear-eyed view of times passed. Here we have a memoir of a long life, well-lived. Many of the poems express the wisdom gained over many years, a summing up of one man's view of the harvest of a productive life. If you enjoy poetry that says what it means and means what it says, then you will delve into this work with pleasure.

-- Sue Scalf, poet.

(Scalf is an award-winning author of nine books of poetry, two of which have been nominated for the Pulitzer Prize. She has been published in numerous literary journals and anthologies and taught English and creative writing at both secondary and university levels.)

"Journey" is my favorite poem of Nathan's. He is an artist with words, for when you read them, life becomes colorfully clear. Nathan Polsky's poems cause us to break free of our usual thinking and to spend just a moment more each day noticing....everything. These poems will live with you for a lifetime.

--Jason Jean, Author and Life Coach

Published By
Suncoast Digital Press, Inc.
www.suncoastdigitalpress.com

ISBN 978-1-939237-05-7

90000 >

9 781939 237057

It Never Hurts To Ask

What is the most important part of your back cover? The answer is *testimonials*. Why does every diet program advertisement include a skinny model saying, "I lost 62 pounds and you can too!" Credibility comes from third parties telling us we should buy the product because they say so, and *they* are not company sales people – they are just like you. Or, they are experts or people with impressive titles, fame, or credentials that give extra credibility to the endorsement. Even if you don't know a potential endorser, it never hurts to ask. In this prime example, the back cover of first-time author Chris Sharek's book, *The Electric Vehicle Revolution*, features a quote from a fellow electric car enthusiast (and world-famous author and celebrity,) Stephen King. It never hurts to ask!

THINKING ABOUT BUYING A HYBRID OR ELECTRIC CAR?

Read this! Written by an environmental engineer, it tells you what you need to know before you shop for your next vehicle.

"In the year my wife and I have been driving our Chevy Volt (136 mpg after 7000 miles), one thought has come to my mind over and over:
"If there were ten million of these on the road in America, life would change. If there were eighty million on the road in America, the budget deficit would disappear, and our dependency on foreign oil would cease. The Volt is, quite simply, the best, sanest car now for sale in America.
Read Chris Sharek's lucid, fact-filled book, and see if you don't agree."

-Stephen King
Steven King, Best-Selling Author and EV Owner

What are municipal decision-makers saying about The Electric Vehicle Revolution?

"The timing of this book couldn't be better. It presents data and information supporting the City's decision to utilize electric vehicles and should serve as an educational resource for future generations."

-Mayor Shirley Groover Bryant, City of Palmetto, Florida

" Sarasota County recognizes the many benefits of alternative transportation and supports local actions to reduce vehicle petroleum consumption. Electric transportation is one strategy that will help reduce our reliance on foreign oil, and with national security, economic, public health and environmental benefits. Thank you for your enthusiasm and initiative in the publishing of a book on electric cars. This may be the wave of the future and your promotion of renewable energy resources is very important. Congratulations for your initiative!"

- Nora Patterson, Sarasota (FL) County Commissioner

Suncoast Digital Press, Inc.
www.suncoastdigitalpress.com

ISBN 978-1-939237-04-0

9 781939 237040

These endorsements are more effective than other promotional words, so be sure and start collecting them early and use them on your back cover. (Extras you collect can be used inside the front pages of the book, on your web site, and other strategic places you will learn about in the chapter on marketing.) Again, the most persuasive testimonials come from a leader or celebrity in your field, sometimes from well-known authors, and also from the raving fan "person on the street" who appreciates what you have to say. It is a well-documented fact that more people will trust and purchase your book when they know that others recommend it.

Bullet Point Your Key Benefits for Readers

What benefits are your target readers going to be most eager to experience? Bullet points are proven to get prospective readers' attention and lead them to read further. Review the research and ideas you had in the earlier process of creating your title and subtitle. The benefits you discovered but didn't capture in the title or subtitle can go on your back cover.

Bring The Reader To Your Web Site

Another key element you can add to the back cover is an enticement to visit your web site. We all want more qualified visitors to our web site, and by including special offers on your back cover you can help sell the book plus build web site traffic. Possible offers include:

"Download FREE Companion Workbook at
www.MyWonderfulBook.com."

"Visit www.MyWonderfulBook.com to take the FREE
Parenting Skills for the 21st Century Self Test."

"Buy this Book and Get the Audio Version for FREE!
www.MyWonderfulBook.com."

Other Elements For The Back Cover

Include a brief author bio – only two or three sentences which make you sound interesting and qualified – and we recommend that authors include a small professionally produced author photo unless there is a good reason to exclude it, e.g., the author is using a *nom de plume*. Don't forget to consider including the name of the illustrator, photographer or designer. Also the back cover is an appropriate place to replicate your book's unique ISBN with bar code, and list the publisher.

How Important Is The Cover To Your Book's Marketing Plan?

- **The cover is featured in advertisements, press releases, catalogs, websites and reviews.** If it is well done, it *will* increase your sales. If it is boring or unconvincing, it *will* detract from your sales.

- **The cover is often the only advertising a book buyer sees.** It is the ultimate point-of-purchase advertising. It either works or it does not. According to the *Wall Street Journal*, the average bookstore browser spends only eight seconds on the front cover – and then only if the reader is attracted enough to pick up the book in the first place. Bookstore owners and publishers have long known that the cover is a point-of-purchase advertisement of major importance in the marketing of the book, and have lavished it with a lot of attention. The same holds true for a digital book cover on your web site or in eBook stores on the Internet.

- **Book covers are also important for advance sales at exhibits or other events.** At an international conference for professional coaches, one executive coach presented a workshop based on her book topic. The book was not yet finished nor published, but she pre-sold 31 copies based on a poster displaying just her book *cover.* Also, social media can be leveraged effectively to pre-sell and announce your book launch… if you have and use your winning book cover on your social media pages.

- **The cover design reflects the professionalism of you as author and your publisher.** If the cover is great, everyone associated with the book makes a good impression. Even book reviewers form first impressions influenced by the cover and will judge if it has been attractively and professionally designed, or if instead reflects a weak or hurried effort.

- **Book covers define a series.** Cover design, when standardized for a series, can help readers to identify other books in the series. Note the standardized covers for the bestselling *Chicken Soup for the Soul* and the *...For Dummies* series. The uniform design of these helps readers to recognize the books as a series. When they buy one and like it, they come back for more.

In this example, "A Little Book of Working Wisdom" is the **series** title. Each book in the series will have the same banner at the top of the front cover, and the same medallion "Steve's 3-Minute Coaching." For the second and subsequent books in the series, the graphics and book title will change, but the consistent elements will tie in all the books which comprise this series. The author planned ahead, creating this first-in-a-series book cover with the appropriate design to carry over in books to follow.

A Little Book of Working Wisdom

PRINCIPLES DISTINCTIONS AND OTHER GEMS FOR

Money Wealth & Freedom

STEVE'S
3-MINUTE
COACHING

Steve Straus

Book Covers: When to Hold Them, When to Fold Them

Your book cover design is a form of packaging and good packaging is a powerful magnet that attracts people to products. While you may be planning to use these tips and design the cover yourself, unless you are experienced in graphic design you may end up with a home-made look that says "amateur" and hurts your chances of success. If you lack talent in this area (and most of us do,) seek the services of an experienced book cover designer who has the skills, high-end page layout software, and creativity that will make your cover stand out as a strong magnet to your target audience, and make you proud of your book's public persona.

Also, by learning the ins-and-outs of book cover design in this chapter, you are prepared to work with a designer in an analytical and informed way that will make your designer's job easier (and perhaps less costly) and enhance the finished product. A great graphic designer may not know all the secrets to great *book cover* design. Your input is important. The simple truth is no matter whether you do it yourself if you have the skills, or hire somebody, your book cover matters throughout the entire marketing program and life of the book.

Key Distinctions For This Chapter

Traditional Book Front/Back Covers vs. eBook "Covers"
A book introduces its subject, tone, genre, and credibility on its front cover. Its back cover clinches the reader's decision to get the book. Even when a reader cannot literally turn a book over to see the back cover, the practice is so ingrained that even eBooks need a front *and* back cover.

Book Cover Artistry vs. Effective Target Marketing Yes, a book is judged by its cover in a matter of seconds, but a beautiful or creatively designed cover does not necessarily translate into the target reader deciding to buy or read the book. The cover must speak to the target reader in tone, style, color, credibility and wording.

Advertising/Promotion vs. Target Marketing/Endorsement While the real estate on the back cover is valuable to help sell the book, it is most effective to use positive endorsement quotes by recognized, named sources or topic-relevant experts rather than simply promotional copy. The recommendations should speak as directly as possible to the book's specific target audience. Other than the testimonial quotes, listing key benefits for your target reader is of highest value.

Summary

Your book cover communicates a world of ideas at a glance – it is far more than window dressing, or bling, or an artistic expression. It truly represents *you* and tells people instantly if your message, your ideas on a topic, are worth their time. Once you have an attractive book cover with all the important elements, you have the ability to consistently make a great first impression. Only then can you hope to draw in your reader like a powerful magnet.

Chapter IX

The Dynamic eBook

Making Your Manuscript
Sing and Dance

What Is A Dynamic Ebook?

Body language. Voice. Cave drawings. Symbols and pictographs. Cuneiform. Alphabet. Books. Illustrated books. This summarizes the evolution of human communication up until present-era technology. But does the technology which gives us email, smart phones, and tablets really give us anything more than the earlier efforts provided, except for speed? When the user/reader has a richer experience because technology was utilized in a meaningful way, then the answer is yes.

In the above abbreviated history of communication, we see that at some point it was agreed that *a word is worth a thousand pictures*. And yet, we still say *a picture is worth a thousand words*. A balance has been reached in many cases by producing printed books which include illustrations or photographs. This helps reader comprehension so much that most all teaching material and text books include a healthy balance of the written word plus visuals. But how many people do you know who have "seen the movie" but never read the book which the movie was based on? Humans crave stimulation of all the senses.

In his international bestseller, *The Hare with Amber Eyes*, Edmund de Waal tells the story of an extraordinary collection of carved Japanese netsuke figurines. Readers were so intrigued they started clamoring to see the objects, so after the hardback, paperback, and eBook versions, the publisher produced a deluxe illustrated edition and also "the enhanced digital edition." The difference in these last two versions is that the enhanced digital edition has the same family photographs, memorabilia, and maps, but also includes embedded videos of de Waal touring readers through the story in Paris and Vienna. The author, a potter with a deep appreciation for the tactile qualities of objects, can be assumed to have hope that the illustrated and enhanced digital editions will give readers a more complete experience of the story he wants to share.

Dynamic eBooks break through the limitations of ink on paper and step up a notch higher in the evolution of ideas in books. Think how much more effectively you could communicate your ideas to your readers if you could infuse your printed pages with elements that brought your ideas to life and caused them to leap off the printed page and right into your reader's mind? What if you could convey your ideas in ways that even the best combination of words, photos and illustrations on the page could not hope to do? What if your ideas and the book you create with them were permeated with video, animation, and sound that drew your reader in and made him or her an active part of the discovery process? That would really make your book a dynamic, active, and almost living entity.

Yes, it can be done! Welcome to the new and exciting world of enhanced, dynamic eBooks.

Enhanced Ebooks Give Authors More Power To Reach Readers

Books, whether electronic or in print, are already remarkable tools of communication. They can teach. They can persuade. They can evoke actions and even emotions. They can take you to faraway places or introduce you to ideas or concepts that you may never have thought to pursue.

The right words have the power to inform and enlighten all by themselves. That is why good writers are so appreciated. But words are not the only thing that should be in books. In the right context, accompanying photographs and illustrations that can be reproduced on the printed page take the author's words and imbue them with a context and meaning that goes beyond what even the most carefully chosen words can accomplish. They also break up large blocks of text on the printed page and make a book more appealing.

Fortunately for us as authors of eBooks, we are not restricted to merely using the printed page and what can be put on it with ink, or its electronic equivalent on a monitor or e-reader. Dynamic eBooks break through the limitations of ink on paper and reach a higher level in the evolution of ideas in books.

This chapter will show you how to create a dynamic eBook (DEB) that will take advantage of state-of-the-art eBook technology. Your dynamic eBook will have the potential to propel your ideas across cyberspace and can engage your readers with a power and ease that you never dreamed possible when you first thought of writing a standard book.

With your dynamic eBook, you will have created a 24/7 soft-sell advocate and advertisement for your business or professional practice with far more marketing clout than the most complete paper brochure or book can offer. In today's competitive world, even publishing a book isn't as meaningful as it once was for the professional to impress their target audience. However, publishing a state-of-the-art eBook is the cutting-edge way to make an indelible impression that you are not only an expert but a leader, someone out in front who readers can admire and trust to be on top of current issues and opportunities.

What Makes A Book "Dynamic"?

What is a dynamic eBook? Generally, something "dynamic" moves and has energy, effective action, and is in itself a force to be reckoned with, so to speak. It is often associated with impact, change, activity, or progress, e.g., a *dynamic market* or a *dynamic public speaker*.

For our purposes, a dynamic eBook (which we refer to as a "DEB" and some others refer to as an "EEB" or enhanced eBook) is an eBook that has a unique energetic quality unlike any regular book or eBook – it can "sing and dance" as a special way of communicating ideas and meaning. In other words, a DEB is an eBook that has its content enriched with state-of-the-art multimedia technology, leveraging available means to enhance important points or key areas.

A DEB is created by taking an ordinary static eBook (one that simply digitizes the printed page) to the next level by infusing its pages with embedded multimedia technology. Think of this as the next step of eBook evolution that leverages existing technology as an effective idea messenger. Forward-thinking authors and corporate marketers are beginning to embrace DEBs not simply because the technology has finally developed to the point where it *can* be done, but because they know it *should* be done to increase the sheer communicating power and impact of their eBooks.

The more you understand the technology and its appropriate uses, the more power these dynamic elements can have. For your completed book to maximize its potential as an enhancement to your personal brand and a success in your target marketplace, it makes sense to think about possible dynamic elements from the beginning of your book development. You should pre-plan where and which dynamic element will have the most impact in your eBook as you flesh out your ideas, create your outline, and begin to write. If you keep these elements in mind throughout the process, your book will incorporate appropriate and useful dynamic elements as needed, and won't appear as though anything was dropped in as an afterthought. Even if you do not plan to embed dynamic elements but simply link to them within the text, you can put QR codes in the text at the appropriate points so a reader can scan even a printed version of your eBook with his or her smart phone and see the dynamic content. Awesome!

You (and your editor or publisher) should think about the best ways that dynamic elements can illustrate and extend your ideas. Once you know what purpose they will serve, where they should be placed, and what form they will take, it is a fairly easy task to create your eBook around and with them. Referring to them in your text and creating cross-referencing hyperlinks back to them will dramatically enhance the power of your eBook. You should also keep in mind that the same dynamic elements you create and put in your eBook can be used more than once. It frequently makes good marketing sense to incorporate them into the state-of-the-art dynamic marketing tools such as a video trailer that you will create and deploy to get your book in front of potential readers once it is published.

What you are doing as you include your dynamic elements as part of your book plan is using savvy author skills which take good advantage of available technology and allow you, as an author and accomplished business professional, to enhance and extend your message and create more reader engagement.

For example, consider the additional information and learning impact that you can create by taking a simple pie chart that you might use as an illustration in your eBook, and transforming it into the lead-in to a dynamic element. If you create and embed audio or video that explains how each piece of pie was derived, and what words mean on each slice of the pie, your pie chart would come alive as an informational element. Or imagine the learning impact of including links to dynamic financial web sites for a book about current affairs' effect on the stock market. Your eBook would essentially constantly change (think of it as changing behind the page) and reflect the implications of your key points. By including a hyperlink that allows the reader to see what is on that web site in real time, you can drive your point home with laser-like impact. Talk about the wow factor!

Practical Dynamic eBook Elements

Should you include some dynamic elements in your eBook? We think the answer is an unqualified "YES" for almost every eBook because they add impact to your ideas and clearly deliver your message to your readers. At a minimum you can add a brief video at the beginning of your eBook of yourself introducing the book – this really helps you connect with readers right from the start. You may have already seen an example in our introductory chapter of this eBook.

There is a trend in children's books, and somewhat in other fiction/novels to leverage multimedia technology for entertainment purposes, meaning that animated characters and videos can enhance the amusement aspect if that is an author's mission. Just as you would expect any child's story to be nicely illustrated, there are more and more book enhancements which readers are learning to enjoy and will soon truly expect.

There is a window of opportunity to be seen as quite impressive by using dynamic elements to spice up your nonfiction work. It's out there, but not yet taken for granted by nonfiction readers. If you are writing a how-to manual of subjects as diverse as contract law, how to exercise properly, a travelogue of a visit to a national park, a book on how to reduce knee pain or even a cookbook, there are many opportunities for effective illustration and demonstration of your points through dynamic elements. In these cases, the information rendered by dynamic elements requires little interpretation by either the creator or the reader. If you are describing a conditioning exercise, for example, a video of somebody doing the exercise with correct form, or an animated drawing of the right posture would be very valuable. Any dynamic element that illustrates and clarifies your ideas and does not detract from them is worth including.

What can be included in a DEB today? The list of potential candidates is as long as you can envision. However, we hasten to add the all-important caveat that envisioning a dynamic element is important—but finding the software to create it, e-readers to render it effectively, and deciding if it enhances your eBook are crucial to consider as you plan your dynamic eBook.

Given the state of present-day eBook authoring tools and e-readers, as well as the technological comfort level of most potential readers of your eBook, it is best to restrict the elements you employ to the typical features that are included in today's web sites and even html-capable email. Using this convention will allow you to take advantage of commonly used, readily available authoring tools. Fear not, this fairly short list is more than feature-rich enough for our purposes and is likely to remain so for a while.

As digital technology develops and reader expectations about dynamic features advance, this list will undoubtedly grow to include many more dynamic elements that we or the legion of "technorati" who create e-readers and eBook authoring software have not yet envisioned, much less written computer programming code to enable.

Which dynamic eBook elements currently make sense is really a matter of the practicality of the technology that is readily available today. Just about any kind of esoteric dynamic element you can envision is probably technically possible to render inside an eBook. All that is required is enough expensive, time-consuming custom programming by the right technical guru, but, is it reasonable to include something at the bleeding edge of technology if your target reader might not even recognize or appreciate it, much less be capable of accessing it? The decision to include any dynamic element in your eBook should be based on the contribution it makes to your message and the reader experience, not on the fact a technical guru could make it work.

Here are the dynamic elements we suggest you might consider using because they are practical to create and are likely to contribute to the idea content of your book. Note that many cannot be rendered by early-generation e-readers, and that they may eat up a great deal of bandwidth. A more detailed discussion appears later in this chapter:

- Video (automatically launched or launched upon an action such as a click.)
- Audio (automatically launched or launched upon an action such as a click.)
- Animated Graphic Interchange Format (GIF.)
- PowerPoint or Prezi (animated and static.)
- Diagnostic tests or Self-Assessments.
- Audio enhanced graphs, charts and diagrams.
- Hyperlinked bookmarks (such as to footnotes) within the text.
- Hyperlinks to outside text, video clips or web-based articles.

Don't Forget Traditional eBook Elements

Just because an eBook element is not strictly dynamic does not mean that it should be ignored. Some traditional elements that can be included on static pages should be considered "honorary" dynamic eBook features in this DEB context as well.

These include photos, illustrations, drawings, Venn diagrams, or bulleted lists.

Even though they are not strictly dynamic per se, they do serve to illustrate and enhance the message of the text and can be effective illustrations and extensions of the above dynamic elements.

These are especially effective when one is placed close to, and serves to further illustrate, a dynamic element in your eBook, or perhaps has a dynamic element associated with it, e.g., a bulleted list or chart with a video or audio "behind" it.

Using Dynamic eBook Elements Effectively

It is useful to think about dynamic elements in an eBook in the same way you think about fonts (Times Roman) or typeface sizes, or styles such as normal, bold, or italic. While there are literally thousands of different fonts and typeface choices available, it makes sense to restrict your choices to a few. Good advice is to use a few, consistently, so your document reads easily and does not look like a ransom note.

As with fonts, if you use too many dynamic elements in your eBook and/or you don't use them with consistency and in a context that the reader can decipher with ease, your enhanced eBook will be cluttered and unappealing. The test is simple: if a dynamic element advances communication and amplifies or clarifies your message to the reader, it makes sense to include it.

Common uses of dynamic elements are to show a dynamic process in action, to illustrate charts and graphs with "behind the scenes" information, to bring the ideas of others to life with a video or audio interview, to demonstrate (even in slow motion) a technique, or to provide examples of what you are writing about.

Here is a link to a short video of an author's testimonial: a dynamic element placed in our chapter about dynamic elements. (In the eBook version of this book of course this is a hyperlink. In this print version, we have embedded a QR code for your convenience.)

OR — if you don't want to view this now, the next time you go to YouTube, look up the Suncoast Digital Press channel where you will find this example and several short videos which are *directly* related to this book.

In your eBook planning and creation, enjoy your modern-day ability to enhance your ideas and spotlight your message through dynamic elements, but don't become so enamored with the technology that you use it wherever you can, rather than where you should.

Creating Dynamic eBook Elements: Technology Harnessed In Service Of Ideas

Okay. You're convinced that creating a dynamic eBook is a great step for you to take as you establish yourself as an in-demand expert and communicate with your present and future customers. So how do you do it?

This section involves some technical discussion, but don't let that deter you if you're not technically-minded. The techniques discussed are simply tools to extend and amplify your communication with readers. You can learn to do the tasks yourself, or let experts do them for you. Either way, what follows is a good way to approach dynamic elements in your eBook. Even if you don't plan on following through yourself, it's good to know what your contracted professionals are doing and why.

First, think very carefully about who your target readers are, and how you will deliver your dynamic eBook to them. If you answer yes to all of the following questions, then the easiest way to put dynamic elements in your eBook is by using tried-and-true web links. There will be no need for special formatting or embedding of your dynamic elements beyond what your html code or PDF creation software can handle. Instead of embedding video in your eBook so it will run offline, for example, you can simply include YouTube video links at the appropriate spots in your dynamic eBook. You can also use hyperlinks to other web sites extensively throughout your document. For this route to prove best, consider:

- Will your DEB be offered only on your web site as an html page or a PDF file?

- Are you certain your target readers are web-savvy and used to going to web sites?

- Will your readers read it only on an Internet-connected device such as a computer, tablet computer hooked to wi-fi, through an App, or a smartphone with a web browser?

- Are you very sure that hosting and selling or giving away your book from your web site(s) will replace any plans to put your DEB on Amazon, Barnes & Noble or other online bookstores that serve up proprietary copy-protected content that is designed to be downloaded to e-readers and read offline?

- Do you have enough good email addresses of your target readers and a concrete marketing plan to reach enough of them to let them know about your book and promote it to them?

- Are you planning to use standard (typical business) software and file extensions so your web visitors can download your DEB and read it on a typical browser of PDF reader?

It is unlikely that you can, or should, answer yes to *all* of these questions. Most of us do not have huge contact lists or web site traffic that can hold a candle to web eBook sales giants like Amazon, Barnes & Noble, or Apple's iTunes. Because each of the different eBook sales site are currently using a proprietary format and unique set of formatting requirements, pre-marketing decisions and manuscript formatting must be addressed at the onset of your eBook creation. As you develop your DEB, you should choose the appropriate dynamic features, insertion techniques, bandwidth requirements for them, and protocols to ensure compatibility with your publishing and marketing plans.

Creating dynamic content is a very rewarding process because you truly achieve a sense of producing something that helps to communicate your ideas with impact as you conceive and build them. Interestingly, the dynamic element creation process frequently has a serendipitous and beneficial effect on your writing because thinking about how you can amplify and clarify your ideas with an illustrative dynamic element causes you to explore your ideas more deeply. Thinking about more than just words causes you to probe what you really mean to convey to the reader as you analyze your ideas and how they are presented. Visualizing these enhancements helps you focus on your readers' experience and how your message will be landing.

Creating Your Dynamic Elements Step By Step

Here are a few tips and techniques to guide you as you create the various kinds of dynamic elements that you will probably want to include in your eBook. Professionals can always be hired to create dynamic elements for eBooks, but may be unnecessary. No dynamic element is so complicated that it cannot be mastered with enough time and motivation.

Creating Dynamic eBook Photographs

Good photographs are not strictly dynamic elements by themselves, but they can be used to good effect alongside true dynamic elements such as video or animation. For example, if you have an audio interview in your DEB, you can use a photo of the interview subject to show your reader who you are talking to.

If you shoot your own photos rather than hiring a photographer, we recommend using a digital camera with at least five megapixel resolution, and shoot it at the highest resolution setting allowed.

Start by reviewing your camera manual if you need to become more familiar with the various features of your specific camera.

Next, consult a good book on digital photography techniques. One of our favorite authors is Scott Kelby but there are others worth reading too.

When you shoot, remember to zoom in close, keep your pictures sharp by using a tripod or a fast shutter speed, and watch your lighting.

As you save the photos, assign a good descriptive name relevant to your project before you manipulate them in the photo-editing software. You will then be able to find them again and it will make it easy to find the insertion placement when formatting your DEB. For example, if your eBook is called *The Secrets of XYZ*, and your photo is of Jo Bob and will go in your second chapter, call your photo XYZ.ch2.Bob. Keep your naming system consistent throughout the book and it will make your life as an author much easier.

If you are having an expert do your final formatting, the easiest way to manage the photos is to include them as attachments when you submit your manuscript and put an editorial instruction or "call out" in red italics with the name of the photo in parentheses in the exact places you want each photo to be placed.

Creating Dynamic eBook Video

Creating really good video is far easier today that it used to be. There are scores of reasonably-priced and very portable high-definition (HD) stand-alone video cameras available. And don't forget that you may already have a great video camera at your disposal since today's crop of digital still cameras (even some for less than $100) can shoot HD video that is simply stunning.

Here is how to do it:

First, consult a good video how-to book. One example is, *How To Shoot Video That Doesn't Suck* by Steve Stockman (New York, Workman Publishing, 2011.) It is available as a print book and eBook. There is even a very useful three-minute video with great tips available on the page of Amazon.com that contains that book's description.

Then watch what the pros do. Noted video author Derrick Story counsels "The cheapest pro- filmmaking course you can take is to park yourself in front of the television and observe how the big guys shoot a scene. Once you start to analyze the work of others, you'll see that good movie-making is often quite fundamental — strong lighting, clear audio, and simple cuts between scenes."

In general, the professionals counsel amateur videographers to limit light sources to a couple, use a white poster board to throw reflected light on the main subject, use ordinary household lamps, or bulbs with clamp-on and plugin reflector fixtures for lighting, avoid or compensate for backlighting, and shade the lens from sun flare. According to film and commercial video professional, Ted Radford, you will have a better result using the new CFL light bulbs for your shoot because you can get a brighter, softer light without all the heat. He also says that whether you buy the "daylight" or "warm indoor" type depends on where you are shooting. If you are near a window and can use the natural light to shine on your subject, then you would use all "daylight" bulbs. If there is very little or no window light, he recommends the "warm indoor" type for all your bulbs. The key is to make sure you have enough light for your camera, and some cameras need less light than others.

Also it is advised to use an external microphone, steady the camera with a tripod or monopod, and shoot fairly short scenes. Stitch them together with simple video editing software that is probably already on your computer or can be downloaded inexpensively or for free.

Plan before you shoot. Decide where you want to shoot your video, who and what will be in it, and then write a simple script. Remember that you are not writing a Hollywood feature-length screen play but just illustrating a point in your eBook so keep your video short and to the point. It can be as short as 30 seconds, and should be no longer than four or five minutes in most cases. Dramatic elements, special effects, background music and fancy camera work are not required.

Try to pick a spot to shoot your video that has a plain background or even blue sky outdoors so background elements don't distract from your message. Watch for distracting shadows on walls too and try to eliminate them by changing your lighting or camera angle. One common problem with an outdoor setting is background noise, so check that.

Plan a simple introduction that introduces the point you want to make and restate the point again in your conclusion. If you are interviewing somebody, have your questions written down. If you are speaking yourself, you don't have to write your script word for word, but simply block out your major points in an outline and talk about the points in a natural conversational tone. Remember that you are the expert so just tell the camera (and your readers) what you know, and what you want them to know about it which is beneficial to them. Just as if you were speaking in front of a room to an audience, pay attention to your voice. Use vocal variety, good energy, and pauses instead of filler words like "so" "um" or "ah".

It is not a good idea to read your script on camera. You can either memorize it or print it out with BIG letters so you can place it next to the camera and read it. No matter which technique you use, be sure to read it or speak in a conversational tone. Imagine your reader is right where the camera is and talk as if you are talking to him.

Next, gather the aforementioned equipment you will need:

- Your camera. Use either a stand-alone video camera (HD is preferred but not absolutely necessary) or a video-capable digital still camera. Microsoft PowerPoint 2010 can also make simple movies that you can use in eBooks. , using a succession of slides to create the illusion of movement. The program has a lot of tools built in to assist.

- If indoors, lamps and other light sources needed, with appropriate CFL bulbs.

- A memory card or other device with sufficient memory to hold the video footage. At least 2 GB of storage capacity is recommended but four or more is better. Depending on the resolution, compression algorithm and frame rate employed, five minutes of HD video requires 1 GB, enough to accommodate 25 minutes of standard video.

- A quality tripod or a monopod to use to steady the camera.

- A piece of white poster board to act as a reflector for illuminating faces or objects that might otherwise be in shadow.

- A good-quality external microphone that plugs into your camera.

Before you shoot the video you use, it is a good idea to shoot some test video so you are familiar with operating your equipment and that your lighting and setting look right. Remember to use the techniques noted here, and that you've picked up by reading books by experts. When you know just a few tips and tricks and use them, your results will improve significantly.

When you are satisfied with how your test videos look, go ahead and shoot the raw footage (unedited video.) If you or your subject makes a mistake speaking, keep going, and shoot the scene or part with the mistake over again. As you edit, it is easy to cut out unwanted parts and keep what is good.

Lastly, use video editing software like the Windows Live Movie Maker or Apple iMovie to put in simple titles, move smoothly from scene to scene, cut out bad scenes, cut the video to the right time length, and perform other simple but important video editing tasks.

There are many more advanced techniques employed by professional videographers that can improve your videos even more, but they are beyond the scope of this overview.

Again, we urge you to think about bandwidth requirements and charges various bookstores may impose for serving large embedded files. Check with your intended bookstores before you set a book price or make the decision to embed large files.

Creating Dynamic eBook Audio

Audio is easier than video, even though it lacks some of video's impact if used in a place where video would be better. Sometimes audio is perfect. You may want to include audio to explain an illustration, graph or photo on a page – the visual is already there so you need an audio not a video element. Also think about audio elements you can include even if you decide not to produce them yourself. You may have access to existing audio clips which fit your content such as a clip from a famous historical speech.

To produce your own audio elements, the first things you will need are a good digital audio recorder and an external microphone, preferably one that is fairly directional, which means it picks up sound only in the direction that it is aimed. (You still have to eliminate background noise as much as possible – loud talking coming from the next room could ruin your results.)

Again, just as with your video, plan and script your audio and prepare questions and introductions for any interviews. Since there will be no video accompanying your audio track, you can even read your script as you go but make sure that you don't rattle papers, tap the table, or disturb the microphone as you record.

The site you choose to record your audio is very important too, especially if you don't have use of a studio. A small, carpeted room usually has better acoustics than a very large room which can pick up echoes. A din of background noise is very distracting unless you are doing a "man on the street" interview. Also, listen before you turn on the microphone. If you hear an appliance, a fan, or other background noises, try to silence them before you record. Without a professional studio, it is not possible to self-edit audio later to keep the voice you want and eliminate unwanted noise. Keep that in mind at the time of recording.

Recording a few test programs before you record the final dynamic audio element is very important. The adage "practice makes perfect" definitely applies to audio recording. It is amazing how many foreign sounds you will hear on your audio before your ear has accustomed itself to listening to "outside" noises; the sounds of everyday life which normally you will not want to include in your audio element.

Once you are satisfied with the purity of the sound quality, make your recording and save it as an mp3 file. You can also make it available as a podcast.

Creating Dynamic eBook Animations

Animated drawings or sequences are both attention-grabbing and powerful illustration tools and, used sparingly, are very good dynamic elements for "How-To-Do-It" eBooks, but should not be used in places where a video would be more effective. A good rule to follow is, if a video of a subject is not possible, then animation is an excellent alternative.

Another very effective tool is using slow motion if you want to show the dynamism and evolution of a complex process or, more generally, any event that occurs so suddenly that the eye cannot fully capture the image.

It is important at this point to mention that producing truly professional animation is complex, expensive and labor intensive. To create animation, many professionals use multiple layers in Adobe Photoshop, while others use more costly professional graphics animation software. If you have the resources, time and interest to learn to use these tools, it is possible to create good animation. However, you will probably want to commission a professional to create animation for your eBook.

If you do decide to attempt the production, there is a less expensive and possibly effective alternative to full professional software: Microsoft PowerPoint and other similar programs have animation features which can be used to produce dynamic elements for your eBook.

Artwork can be created by using the program's AutoShape features. By using the "custom animation" features built into a PowerPoint slide show, art work can be animated slide-by-slide.

Another useful tool is Power Point is "transitions" which offers ways of producing simple fade-in/fade-out effects for slides or video.

Indeed, there are a myriad of useful software and animation tools available for use in creating dynamic effects in your eBook. Still, we advise authors to avoid succumbing to the lure of technology for its own sake, and to be aware of the size of the final DEB they are creating by inclusion of dynamic elements. We also advise using professionals for complex multimedia tasks to make sure the quality is high and your project stays on schedule.

Creating Dynamic eBook Hyperlinks

Words in a manuscript can be encoded with a specific Internet site address so that a reader using an electronic means to read the words can click on the word(s) and automatically leave the page and go to the linked site. These "hyperlinks" are among the most used and most-appreciated features of Internet technology. By creating a DEB version of your book, you will be able to take full advantage of this dynamic tool to create a link to other sites anywhere on the Internet.

The downside of the hyperlink is that your reader is being transported out of your eBook site to another destination. You run the risk that she will find the content of where you send her so compelling that she will not return to your eBook. With that awareness, use hyperlinks carefully. Another approach is to only use links to pages on your own web site – locate the additional information your reader chooses to view there.

If your eBook, like most published, is intended to be read with an e-reader rather than just on a website, the best use of hyperlinks is to make them function as bookmarks. You can send your reader to a footnote or another reference or dynamic illustration on the same topic by creating a bookmark within your eBook using the bookmark feature in the software you are using (such as Microsoft Word) to create your manuscript. Bookmarks can also be used in PDF documents.

Michael Wong (http://www.great-web-design-tips.com) offers the following hyperlink tips that also apply to bookmarks. He suggests using action links that "Where possible, always name links in terms of user actions." For example, 'Go to Checkout' is preferred to 'Checkout', 'View Cart' is preferred to 'Shopping

Cart' and 'Check Email' is preferred to 'Email' as the title of your hyperlink or bookmark. Don't hesitate to tell your reader exactly what to do.

Like any other dynamic element, too many hyperlinks can distract rather than inform. Use hyperlinks only when you determine that your reader visiting an Internet site, such as your YouTube channel, will further clarify your book's message, demonstrate a point, and add value to the reader. Another appropriate place to use bookmark hyperlinks is in your table of contents so your reader can jump right to the chapter he wants to read.

Before you submit your manuscript, check to verify that each hyperlink and bookmark work properly. Then check them all again!

Key Distinctions For This Chapter

Dynamic or Enhanced vs. Standard eBook   Technology and user expectations, especially in the rapidly-growing use of video, have affected eBook design, development, and use. Standard eBooks are still excellent vehicles to produce as digital versions of your book in order to meet the market demand of millions of people who prefer to read books on e-readers or other devices. Dynamic eBooks are enhanced versions which include multimedia elements such as video, audio or animation, and are a growing trend.

Director vs. Producer   To produce the dynamic elements and have them work flawlessly in your eBook requires technical skill, large amounts of time, special software, and upgraded equipment (an HD video camera, for example,) and then a course of study in conversion processes for each necessary format to have your book be compatible with Amazon, Barnes & Noble, Apple and other reading devices. In most cases it is better for the author to make the decisions about which multimedia features make sense, write down what they want the result to look like, and then direct other experts to produce them.

Summary

EBooks, to most of us, seem like "new technology." The fact is that they, and the devices people use to read them on, are evolving at a rapid pace. The standard eBook now outsells printed books on Amazon, but readers are starting to expect more exciting features in their digital books. Multimedia enhancements make some eBooks "sing and dance" and you will see these eBooks described as "enhanced eBooks" (EEBs) or "dynamic eBooks" (DEBs.)

For your completed book to maximize its potential as an enhancement to your personal brand and as a success in your target marketplace, it makes sense to think about possible dynamic elements from the beginning of your book development. You should pre-plan where and which dynamic element will have the most impact in your eBook as you flesh out your ideas, create your outline, and begin to write. Unless you are eager to tackle a steep learning curve, you'll want to study this chapter and other resources, understand why and what you want your DEB to do, and (most likely) have other people with specialized experience handle the production.

Chapter X

Transforming A Manuscript Into An EBook

Using Technology To Reach Your Target Readers

Digital Publishing: The Technical Environment

There is a point in time where you can take off your author's hat and put on your self-publisher's hat. You have traveled a long way now from where your journey started when you decided to write a book. You have identified an audience, selected a title, and spent hours crafting you message. Now you have actually completed the book and have decided on any illustrations, photos, or graphics to include, and probably some dynamic elements for the eBook version which will enliven your manuscript. It is time to select the tools which will help you complete the step that actually creates a published eBook and any derivative Print-On-Demand (POD) copies you ultimately require.

Are you old enough to remember the competition between the Beta and VHS formats back in the early days of video recording? A similar contest between competing eBook publishing formats is underway today.

The formats themselves (how the eBook is created in computer code so that a reader's Nook, Kindle, iPad, or other device can read it) and the underlying book industry standards that drive those technical formats is being vigorously debated by industry leaders.

Why is this important to you as an author? The answer is that different readers in your target audience are using different devices when they download and read books electronically, so you have to produce as many different formats as necessary to accommodate as many of the popular devices as possible. You don't want to lose a prospective reader when it is avoidable by following the information in this chapter and in other chapters in this book.

The major brand e-readers (Kindle, Nook, Adobe Reader and Apple, plus several others) all require different "renderings" (digital conversions of your manuscript.) That's right – there is no industry standard today and none is expected in the near future.

The software tools you select to create the various versions your audience will use can be very challenging to obtain and master. Once you do obtain and master them, you can use them to create the versions that allow your audience to view your book on their e-reader, and then to take advantage of the multimedia capabilities that you the author may want your audience to experience.

There are many such devices on the market, and these e-readers (technically called "renderers") are evolving very rapidly, following the usual technology trend of becoming more powerful, feature-rich, and more affordable simultaneously. While this is great news for consumers, it is not such good news for authors and publishers. The big catch for authors and eBook publishers is that since there is no industry standard, we must consider that fact as we search for and evaluate which tools to use in publishing. Our goal is to make our information products more accessible to the readers we are targeting no matter which electronic reading device they own.

So, there is no "one-size-fits-all" and no such e-reader is likely to emerge in the short term. Not all formats allow all the capabilities of a given manuscript to come through. To make things even more difficult for the author, *there is no universal conversion tool to render a word-processed manuscript into a universally-readable eBook*. No conversion software does all formats equally well, and some only work with one or two formats. In the long run, the industry may not need multiple formats, but certainly for the short run, and very probably for at least the next several years, we will be dealing with those tricky multiple formats.

Key Considerations For Selecting The Right Publishing Tools

You are wisely bypassing the old-fashioned traditional and slow publishing companies to alternatively self-publish and maintain much more control, but does it make sense for you to take on the complex job of converting your manuscript into publishing formats for various technical devices?

The answer is that it depends on how you resolve some important considerations: if you pay for a service rather than do it yourself, is there a catch such as whether you have to surrender a percentage of your sales? Are you restricted to offering your book *only* in the service provider's book store? Will you have to use more than one vendor to get all the formats you need?

If you choose to format your eBook for publication yourself, you also need to know what software is available today, what kind of manuscript formatting and file type is required, how hard and expensive is it to use, and whether a given piece of conversion software or combination of them will accommodate the various e-readers in your audience. If you have dynamic elements, you must verify that the software and target hardware can accommodate all the multimedia capabilities you want to include.

The All-Important Publishing Tool

All publishing software is not the same. Just as e-readers have various capabilities and limitations, so too are the publishing tools subject to these same variations. For example, some publishing tools can handle photos or video synchronized with audio, while others may not be capable of handling the audio and/or files at all. Still others may not retain the synchronization of these dynamic elements.

Generally, publishing tools break down into two categories: those which can offer an integrated solution and those which do not.

Integrated publishing tools strive for a complete set of publishing capabilities for the self-publishing author. Typically they provide a text editor or word processor for preparing written text. Some also include the capability of storing and embedding the dynamic material in the written material as part of the eBook content. Many do not allow dynamic content, and the ones that do can have differing requirements for including dynamic material. They also usually provide a library capability for storing and managing the content you create. Also they are capable of publishing the final content by producing output that is capable of being rendered on various readers, some more effectively than others. Most are highly proprietary and you can lease the use of them for a fee, or through paying a certain percentage of the revenue you earn as you sell books.

Other publishing tools do not attempt to provide integrated functionality. They focus on the embedding of the dynamic content and publishing steps only. Other applications are used in conjunction with them to provide the capabilities necessary to create your eBook. Adobe Acrobat (full version, not the Reader,) Calibre, Jutoh, Kindlegen and Sigil are popular among the current crop of software tools but new competitors and versions are likely to enter the marketplace as eBooks become more ubiquitous.

Each approach has its advantages and disadvantages. One major plus for the integrated approach is that all the capabilities needed to produce your eBook are gathered in one place. But the disadvantages are that authors must learn how the tool functions, surrender some of their earnings, and work within time-consuming and exacting limitations in formatting and manuscript presentation.

Alternatively, the stand-alone approach usually has the advantage that the scope of the publishing tool is limited and therefore can be more easily learned. Yet it too will have limitations which the author must learn to work around and, of course, it will only produce files that are readable on a limited number of rendering devices. You must learn how to integrate the eBook content using the variety of tools you have selected for this task. Also, when you are using dynamic content, these elements must be embedded technologically after the text has been completed. You can't just drop in photos, videos, and so forth as you would in a word-processed document and expect them to work in an eBook.

Frankly, unless you are willing to acquire and become proficient with often-complex and expensive publishing tools, you are better off hiring an expert to create your ready-to-publish eBook from your manuscript, or work with a publisher that provides that service.

Targeting Your eBook Display Device

Renderers (the display devices on which a given eBook is presented) are more commonly known as e-readers. Some of the more popular e-readers today include the family of Barnes & Noble *Nook* devices, the many Amazon *Kindle* devices, Apple's *iPods*, *iPads*, and *iPhones*, the Sony readers, Google's platforms, the burgeoning array of tablet computers on the market and many others.

It is essential that you understand the behavior of the e-readers you are targeting for your specific eBook manuscript because each e-reader handles text and dynamic material differently and, in most cases, what can be viewed on a Nook cannot be viewed on a Kindle and vice versa. There are also software renderers/readers available from many sources, for example Microsoft and Adobe, *The New York Times*, as well as many others. These software applications function on PC's and Mac's and allow you to read various file formats such as epub (Nook, for example) or mobi (Kindle, for example.) The broader the intended reading audience, the more likely it is that most of the renderers mentioned will be used by at least some of your potential readers. In other words, your eBook needs to be created in many different file formats to increase the likelihood that your target readers will be able to read your eBook on the device they use. (This is also why most authors offer a paper-printed version to satisfy certain consumers.)

The display areas and their proportions vary from model to model even within the same brand and e-reader family. Some units display only black and white, while others include impressive color capabilities. Some can accommodate video while others do not, and only some recent models are capable of color video and sound. Another important capability (or limitation) is the image resolution of the device. Some older models present very grainy images on the screen while newer models handle fast action video and high-resolution photos without video stuttering or image distortion.

The Apple series of display devices (iPad and iPhone) have dominated their markets over the past two or three years. And, there is currently no reason to believe that this trend will change in the near future. Specifically, the iPad tablet is the best-selling unit in its category and makes a great eBook display device for some formats. It is also widely used by business people and professionals. So, when targeting renderers for your eBook, it would be wise to consider this manufacturer's products in your plans. But Amazon Kindle, especially, and Barnes & Noble also have huge audiences and need to be taken into account as well.

E-reader sales in 2013 are expected to top 14 million and eBook sales are predicted to jump from 323 million in 2008 to 9 *billion* this year.

Product sales numbers do not tell the whole story because reliable statistics measuring the amount and purpose of use for display devices are not available. So even though the Apple devices are extremely popular, it is almost certainly true that the Amazon and Barnes & Noble e-readers have been primarily used for reading eBooks, whereas Apple's are used for many things including reading eBooks, surfing the web, gaming, and email.

Nearly every day there is news in the publishing industry on this topic, so you would be smart to check for updates if you have a question about this subject. For example, now you can download an App for your Apple iPad which allows that device to act like a Kindle, allowing you to read eBooks from the Kindle Store.

The trend which will continue to grow, and inevitably dominate the world's reading habits, is that reading content will be rendered by electronic display devices. One format will probably become dominant in the long run. Which one it will be, however, is impossible to say with certainty as of this writing. If you are going to publish an eBook and hope to reach a broad market in the foreseeable future, you will need to accommodate many different e-readers and publish your eBook in several appropriate formats.

Document Format And File Storing Decisions Are Important

Careful attention must be given to the file formats that you use to create your eBook content. There are two major considerations here: the publishing tool you choose, and the target eBook renderers/e-readers you are trying to reach.

Looking at the target renderers, we have already emphasized that not all e-readers are capable of handling all file formats. In fact no renderer available on the market today is capable of handling all the file formats that are in common use. In most cases, the format standard used by manufacturers of eBook renderers/e-readers for interpreting content does not truly conform to the current epub 3 "standard". This standard defines the file formats (as well as many other things) which all renderers should be able to handle when displaying eBook content. Unfortunately, it is more of a goal than a standard, and is not an effective format in today's real-world of eBooks and e-readers.

What this all means for you, the author, is that if an eBook is published in formats readable by several different renderers, the content displayed on each device could easily be displayed differently on each machine. And it is entirely possible that on some of the renderers the display process could fail totally, perhaps only displaying an error message, or perhaps displaying nothing at all.

Consider, too, the publishing software used to produce an eBook from a text or PDF manuscript. There are a great variety of publishing tools available in the marketplace and there is an equally wide range of capabilities and limitations associated with them. The publishing tool or tools you select must be capable of properly producing your eBook content on all display devices likely to be used by those you target for your readership. The wider your intended audience, the more likely it will be that your eBook will be viewed on a myriad of incompatible devices.

Do I Need to Use the ISBN System?

To help to protect, identify, distribute and track your eBook, you should understand and use the ISBN system to make your book more professional and marketable.

Taking an excerpt from the ISBN system as it is described in the ISBN User Manual:

The International Standard Book Number (ISBN), known throughout the world, is an identification number that is assigned to an individual book or eBook and it is the equivalent of a Vehicle Identification Number (VIN) of an automobile. It marks a book unmistakably and identifies it to the world. Whenever intellectual products are covered by a numbering system, the International Standard Book Numbering designation should be used. ISBN, ISSN, ISMN, ISSN are examples of classes within the overall numbering system. The ISBN classification is commonly applied to books and, once assigned, stays with the book from its production, through publication and for the life of the book.

It is an essential instrument in modern distribution and tracking in the book trade and we strongly advise that each eBook or book you publish should have its own ISBN. While it is not absolutely required, it has so many advantages that the fairly nominal cost of securing an ISBN makes it worthwhile by a substantial margin. Once you obtain your unique number (we use Bowker Identifying Services but your publisher usually obtains one for you,) you can get a bar code graphic image which most authors put on their book's back cover. You may need a version which includes the retail selling price — check your intended bookseller's requirement specifications.

The word "book" is used in the ISBN User Manual in the sense of content or "publication." Therefore, it is of no importance which physical form this content takes and is distributed. What is important is that each distinct form should have its own ISBN. If you have a printed book with an ISBN assigned to it, you will still need a separate ISBN for your eBook because it is considered a separate publication by most book distributors. There is some disagreement within the industry whether each type of eBook, e.g., epub, mobi, PDF, and so forth, requires its own ISBN, but the prevailing opinion as of this writing is that one ISBN can apply to all of your eBook format versions as long as the content remains exactly the same.

The unique international identifier that is an ISBN is very useful to authors, publishers, and the whole book trade because the thirteen-digit number replaces the handling of long bibliographic descriptive records throughout the industry. Time and staff are saved, copying mistakes are avoided, and your book gains instant credibility.

Copyright and Copyright Registration: Protecting Your Intellectual Property

In general, a copyright typically protects an original artistic or literary work such as a book. Copyright registration is a legal formality intended to make a public record of the basic facts of a particular copyright. Information about it can be found at The US Copyright Office site at the copyright.gov web site. *However, registration is not a condition of a substantial degree of copyright protection.*

The above sentence notwithstanding, registration under the copyright law provides several inducements or advantages to encourage copyright owners to complete the registration process. Among these advantages are:

- Registration establishes a public record of the copyright claim.

- Before an infringement suit may be filed in court, registration is necessary for works of U.S. origin.

- Registration allows the owner of the copyright to record the registration with the US Customs Service for protection against the importation of infringing copies.

- Registration of a copyright automatically registers a book with the Library of Congress. However, registration does not guarantee the cataloguing your book by the Library for its permanent collection. A Library of Congress Card Catalog Number is assigned by the Library at its discretion to assist librarians in acquiring and cataloging works.

Again, registering your copyright is an optional step you can take, but know that "copyright" refers to your ownership of *original* material and is *automatic* – if you created it yourself you automatically have copyright protection on it.

Here is how to write your own copyright notice on your work: First, you can use the symbol © which is the letter "C" in a circle, or you can spell out the word "Copyright" and then follow this with the year of first publication. The third required element is the name of the owner of copyright, or an abbreviation by which the name can be recognized. Example: © 2013 Jane Doe

Since we are not attorneys and are not dispensing legal advice, we recommend consulting an attorney with copyright and intellectual property expertise before you make any decisions about copyright.

Video or original music which you hire someone to produce or create yourself (which includes only original material – not taping a band performing at a concert, for example) falls under the automatic copyright protection whether you embed the video or audio in your eBook, use it on your own web site or upload it to your YouTube channel. Again, for more information about the Internet and copyright law, the "Digital Millennium Copyright Act" or for more details about US Copyright registration, visit the official US government web site at or consult a qualified attorney.

You should also be familiar with what lawyers call "fair use," e.g., the right of reviewers, researchers and others to quote short pieces of your work regardless of copyright level. Again, consult an attorney on the meaning and applicability of fair use whether you are quoting or being quoted in any specific circumstances.

POD: What about Print-On-Demand Services?

In addition to your eBook versions, do you want printed copies of your book? With today's digital technology, it probably makes sense to have both eBook and printed versions of your work. It's quite feasible to do both. Print-On-Demand (POD) is a publishing and distribution option that many writers choose because it allows authors to take advantage of digital printing vs. traditional printing press technology and have their book available to print and bind literally one at a time or in small quantities. POD is a book production method whereby books are printed only as ordered, and usually in small quantities per order. Due to the capabilities of digital printing, it is no longer necessary to rely on high volume to make producing a book affordable. Now it is reasonably practical to order and produce one or a few books at a time if large volume printing does not make sense.

This innovation is of significant importance to self-publishing authors because it gives you much more control and many more affordable options than "vanity presses" or large traditional publishers have provided. POD is a fairly new and excellent option that allows you to avoid having to order a huge number of books, incur considerable up-front costs, and deal with the burdens of inventory and shipping. A reader who wants a printed book rather than an eBook can order one easily through a link provided by the author or bookseller.

For the author's own desired inventory, POD is the convenient way to purchase a few printed-on-paper, bound copies of the book to use for promotional and marketing purposes, or to sell at places he/she plans to appear in person. Although there are a growing number of success stories where a self-published book is picked up by a large publishing house which would then commit resources to producing large quantities, POD is the best method for most self-publishers to count on and include in their distribution and marketing plan.

Keep Your Eye On The Goal

It is wise to remember that your completed book is a means of sharing your message, enhancing your credibility in your marketplace, and reaping other rewards which come from being a published author: you will *not* increase your impact or business because you have learned publishing steps such as how to produce Nook-compatible dynamic elements. You should understand the processes in this and other chapters, not overspend your personal time mastering the sometimes-very-technical demands of each step.

Once you have completed this book's first ten self-publishing chapters you will have your book ready for the world. Amazon, Barnes & Noble and other top online eBook sellers will accept your correctly formatted manuscript (with rare exception) and... you're in business!

Key Distinctions For This Chapter

Formatting a Document vs. Formatting a Manuscript for Publication   From experience typing in word-processing software (such as Microsoft Word) you know certain formatting tasks are required to produce a professional looking document: margins, font styles and sizes, headers/footers, and page-numbering are examples. This is not true when preparing your document for publication in forms various e-readers can use – this preparation demands an entirely different set of rules, not only different from MS Word, but different from one another.

Generally Popular E-Readers vs. Your Target Reader's Preference   In your early research to identify and describe your book's ideal target reader, you may not have determined how these readers opt to consume books. Before publishing in various formats, you need to know if your target reader owns the latest Apple device, the least expensive, limited capability e-reader, or strongly prefers to hold a paper-page bound book in his/her hands.

Automatic Copyright vs. Registered Copyright
"Copyright" refers to your ownership of original material and is automatic – if you created it yourself and add a notice that your material is copyrighted, you automatically have copyright protection on it. When you go through the application process with the US Copyright office to register your copyright, you establish a public record of your copyright claim and gain some additional protection.

Summary

Writing your manuscript and being satisfied with the final editing and proof-reading last steps has led you to another door, another stairway where your first steps of *publishing* begin.

"Formatting" a document is preparing your manuscript so it can be published and distributed for various e-reading devices or printed-on-paper versions. It is far more technically involved than simply formatting a word-processed document.

How many different formats should be generated depends on the readers you wish to reach. Fortunately, it is possible to accommodate just about everyone, including readers who want a "real book" which can be easily provided through the practical publication and distribution option, Print-On-Demand.

Other considerations before publishing your book include determining your desired copyright protection and obtaining an ISBN.

Chapter XI

Marketing: The Book/EBook Success Secret

The Author's Reward: Achieving Readership

There are tens of thousands of books published each month worldwide. Many are quite good and deserve both recognition and rewards for their authors. Unfortunately, only a very tiny fraction of them garner sufficient readers to repay their hard-working authors with the recognition they deserve or the sales they want. Most published authors toil in anonymity and never attract enough readers or make enough sales to compensate them for the time they have invested and the creativity they have poured into their magnum opus. Indeed, *the world's best mousetrap* is not enough to catch a mouse. Your book must be positioned with high visibility to your target audience, communicate at a glance the benefits or promise they will respond to, and be easy enough to pick up and start reading.

While this chapter often uses the term "sales" to measure a book's success, our recommended approach is designed to *attract* your target audience and secure a commitment. Whether they make a purchase or download a free copy, they must be sold on the idea it will be worthwhile to read your book. There are many proven strategies to make your book as attractive as a powerful magnet – a magnet directed to your ideal target readers. This chapter will teach you how to understand and employ these strategies.

Luck and timing do play some role in success, but the main driver that separates the successful from the not-so-successful book is a 21st century marketing strategy which is applied before the book is even published. Did you know there are at least five things you should be doing *now*, even before your book is finished, to put your book on the fast track to reaching your goals? This is what makes this book – and this chapter – so contemporary and valuable. You also will learn how to power your book launch with a marketing blitz upon publication, and how to systematically build sales over the long haul with a continuous and customized marketing program. EBooks especially need a great marketing plan because they are digital products and can get lost in the huge and growing expanse of the World Wide Web and its giant online bookstores. On the Amazon web site alone, there are nearly three million eBooks available. Yours will not stand out unless you stand up and actively market it. Let's get started.

Five Book Marketing Actions To Take *Before* Your Book Is Published

Have you read your book mission statement and reviewed your personal goals for your book today? Do you have your attention-grabbing title and subtitle? Believe it…you are soon to become a published author! As you begin to think that way, and speak that way, you will naturally find many opportunities to share this good news with the world. Here are some ideas, plus, if you think about it, you can come up with many others as well.

- **Enhance your email signature** by adding, after your name, "Author of the forthcoming book, "_____ "
- **Find your name!** Where do you currently have a bio or profile? Add the news about your book to your bio on your web site, your speaker's introduction, Linked-In profile, blog byline, listing on your professional networking group's web site, and anywhere people will find information about you.
- **Write/Rewrite your "elevator speech."** This simply means it is time to update your personal introduction – your audio logo – which is the carefully crafted thirty-second message you develop and memorize so you can confidently and consistently tell people who you are. Insert the fact that "I am the author of the book _____, or, the forthcoming book _____ " and then give one big benefit, i.e., the *why* someone should read your book.
- **Create a special business card** for your book. Once you have your book cover, use the graphic image to start promoting your book. ("Vista Print" is one web site which guides you through producing a custom business card easily and inexpensively.) When you have a business card with your book cover image featured, you are able to easily pass out the good news to everyone you meet. And don't limit it to the paper

version! Get creative with a virtual business card, with or without an audio clip.

- **Create a video book trailer**. Once you have your book title and an image of your book cover, you should create a video book trailer. It is usually a well-produced and short (two minutes or less) clip which sometimes includes an author interview and shows the reader what is in it for them. Proficiency with videography and video editing is recommended if you are going to create it yourself. Otherwise, hire a professional to create one for you. Check out this example:

OR — if you don't want to view this QR code with your smartphone free App now, the next time you go to YouTube, look up the Suncoast Digital Press channel where you will find this example and several short videos which are *directly* related to this book.

First-time author, Chris Sharek, used the above video to help build excitement and interest in his book before it came out and, of course, leverages it now on his own web site and in his ongoing marketing strategy.

If you have already published a book and are just now starting to think about marketing, perhaps because you did not realize how much the promotion is completely up to you, you can start with the above actions and continue to build on them.

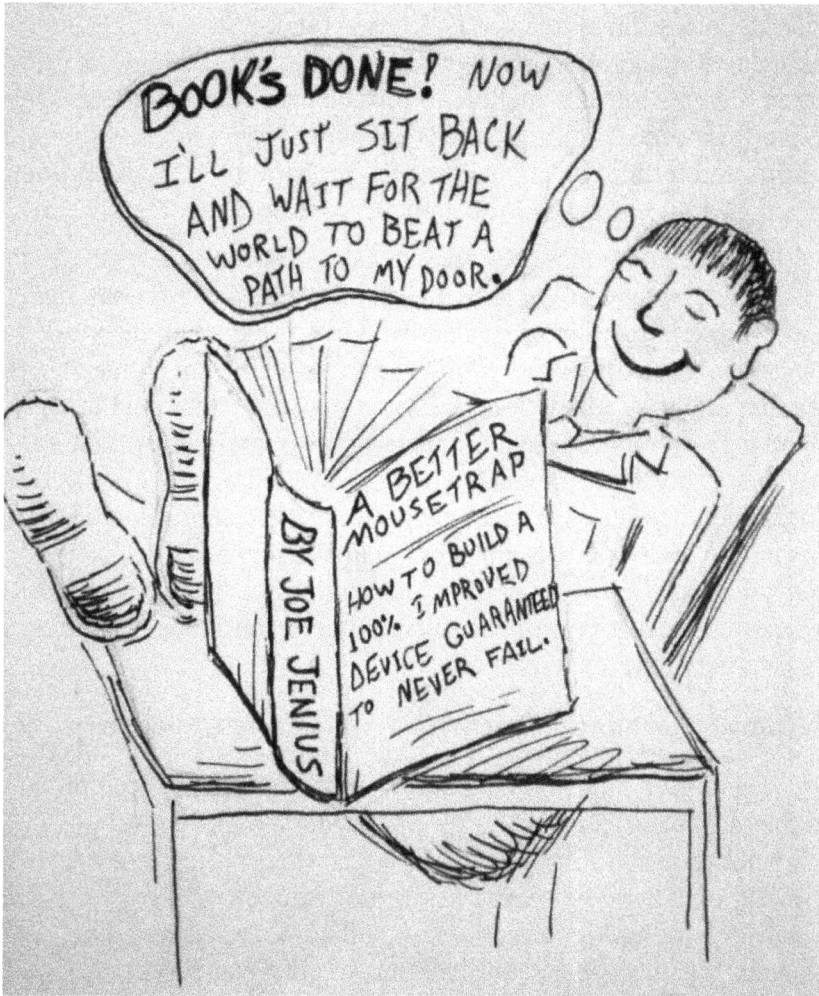

Sales And Marketing Scaled For The Self-Publisher

Once your book is produced, it is time to invest your energy and implement your best ideas to persuade readers to read it. Yes, you need to *sell* your book.

Selling a product like a book is a commercial exchange. You attract the potential customer, let her/him know about your book, show how much it costs, agree to a transaction where you provide the book and your customer provides you with money. If you plan to provide your book for free as part of your marketing strategy to connect with potential clients, everything about "sales" in this chapter does still apply to you because you need to *sell* a reader on taking action, i.e. obtaining and reading your book. Many marketing experts also include follow-up customer service as part of the sales process since it keeps customers happy (preventing returns and refunds) and increases the probability they will become repeat customers and will recommend your book to others.

But sales do not happen in a vacuum. They exist in the environment made possible by marketing, which is a far broader term. Marketing is a process that evaluates the marketplace to identify what people want, who the people who want a given product might be (demographics,) and how they think and feel about a given topic (psychographics.) It also involves evaluating whether you want to produce a product like a dynamic eBook for a given audience (marketplace) and, ultimately, establishing and expanding your brand as a professional and published author. Marketing also involves pricing, packaging (the book cover and promotional description,) and positioning to showcase the value to your target niche customers.

Become Irresistibly Attractive To Your Target Audience

There is an exceptional kind of marketing that we recommend as the most effective method for promoting independently published nonfiction books and eBooks: *Attraction Marketing*. It is sometimes called reverse marketing or magnetic marketing because if you use it correctly, you will attract customers like a magnet. It is the opposite of hard-sell, aggressive marketing because, according to a *Wikipedia* article, it "uses techniques specifically designed to teach the customer what you are doing and how a service or product will benefit them well before they purchase it....providing valuable content for potential customers to figure out how your product is going to benefit them before they buy it so that they are qualified customers before they step in the door." Generating high-value perception is highly attractive and pulls readers in like a magnet.

The *Attraction Marketing* model is one that is generous rather than only self-serving. When applied to marketing a nonfiction, professional book, an effective attraction-principle technique is to put free information with real value such as special reports, sample chapters, and other useful nuggets on your web site and publicize it to your email list. (More about your list later in this chapter.) By providing some of what is expanded upon in your book, you are building trust and offering something of solid value at no charge, thereby creating an environment where people are predisposed to purchase your books because they have enough confidence to go for more of what you have to offer. You are persuading them to believe that the information in the next level of products or services will be even more beneficial than what they have already received.

Just Try One Bite...

The idea is to make a connection, no matter how fleeting it may seem at first, with a person who matches as perfectly as possible with the profile of your ideal client or customer. The beauty of the Internet is that you can reach so many people so easily, yet its downfall is that relationships are harder to start and cultivate online due to the impersonal nature of interacting with a screen instead of a real person. **Like a free sample of ice cream**, just a taste of what you are able to serve up can go a long way in establishing more of a connection with your ideal client.

The five main ingredients in your one-bite customer lure:

1. **Free.** The spirit of the magnetic marketing offer is that it is given freely by the author in exchange for the potential customer's time and effort in giving their contact information such as when you put a free excerpt of your eBook on your web site. You can also give away a free excerpt in the Amazon Kindle store, or offer your eBook for the first 72 hours after launch for no charge.

2. **Compelling**. The more the information is close to something your target reader is "desperate to know" and not just mildly interesting, the better. You've attracted their attention – now don't miss the opportunity to connect by failing to elicit emotion and strong interest. Don't be boring.

3. **Bite-sized.** A relatively small sample can have a great effect without giving away too much. Make it easy for someone to say "Yeah, sure I'll try a little bite." Also, you want the potential customer to still be curious, hungry for more now that they have had a sample. Don't overpromise or give away anything that costs you too much of your valuable time or effort.

4. **Keep it simple.** You should be able to create your free marketing magnet in a day or less. You may already have it developed and simply need to package it, like the example of giving away one chapter of your book. The give-away must stand on its own once placed as your free offer, not require your time on an on-going basis.

5. **Natural to your brand.** Make your free sample the first step on the path you want the customer to follow straight to the door of your primary service or product. For example, a luxury cruise site could give away a free eBook about which ports and cities are currently the safest for world travelers and why. Position your first connection to serve as an introduction to your core business.

Find Your Audience And Turn The Spotlight On

Attraction Marketing is not a passive, magic "just show up and be generous" formula. First you must define your niche market, also known as a group of people with common issues or concerns. Next you have to discover where your potential customers are probably spending time. Then, based upon this information, you can make your website, your blog, social media posts and appearances both highly visible and engaging. It is not a "build a great info-freebie and they will come" process. You must make it easy for people to find you and sell themselves on you and your information. If you think about **value** and are generous with information you share, you will be on the right track.

Once you have introduced yourself and exchanged your free gift for a person's contact information, the next level of relationship building is when you successfully persuade them to read your book.

Market research shows that there are various levels of buying resistance that people tend to have when making a purchase decision. When you attract a customer to try you for free, you are overcoming the first resistance level and have successfully drawn them into your world. When you attract them with your book or dynamic eBook to check out your knowledge and credibility, you have successfully drawn them into your next level of service/product opportunities. They are starting to buy in to your brand. Each step of the way you are providing more value and they are spending more money.

"You Are Cordially Invited …To My List"

Doesn't it feel easier to start a list of people you would like to invite as guests to a party you are giving than a list of target prospects? "Target" makes it sound like you're lining them up for a firing squad. You need a list and of people who are interested in what you produce, and you need to be motivated to build it and use it. Start and maintain a list of those who have shown that interest by visiting your web site and registering, or otherwise have expressed an interest.

Following *Attraction Marketing* principles will give you confidence that your list will be used to inform people rather than sell them. Most of us want to be sure we are not coming across as "pushy" or "only interested in making a sale." Professional Sales is an honorable profession, certainly, but *being sold* has a lot of negative and unpleasant associations attached. One useful distinction to make is between "enroll" and "sell." You enroll someone when you stand next to them, figuratively speaking, and you look at the offer together to see if it's a match for what is wanted and needed. A person is interested, and then enrolled into making a decision, when they get a strong sense of *what's in it for them.* People like to buy, but do not like to be sold. Especially in today's marketplace, people are almost allergic to being sold anything, and respond much more positively to *Attraction Marketing.*

If you follow these principles as you build and use your list, you can proceed with the confidence that it will be used to share valuable information which will be of benefit to them, and keep you in touch with your clients and contacts.

Where Preparation Meets Opportunity: Finding Luck In List-Building

You have the ability to communicate with an unlimited number of people because almost everyone has an email address which enables you to get your message out to huge segments of the market with absolutely no advertising, printing, or mailing expenses. This is unprecedented and if we approach this opportunity correctly, it is highly effective for book marketing and business building.

If you haven't already started a special email group to collect addresses for your book marketing list, set one up. Include all your existing contacts. If you aren't sure whether someone would want to be on your list, remember that you will never send high-pressure sales jargon, and that when you do send a magnetic marketing message, the recipients will have a choice to stay on your list, or not. "Opt-In" is a term which means a person has to subscribe (sign up) and indicate they want to continue receiving your emails. "Opt-Out" means they are automatically subscribed until they exercise the option to unsubscribe. Either method can work; it really depends on your comfort level. Once you have a few contacts from your own address book added into your list, where else can you find contacts to build your list?

There are scores of ways to target potential customers so you can get your information in front of them, win them over, and turn them into what management guru and best-selling author, Ken Blanchard, calls "raving fans."

Think about the following groups of people and make lists so you can email them, talk to them, hand them a business card if you see them face-to-face, or otherwise get something in front of them that will let them know about your book and its benefit to readers. Here are a few list-building tips:

First-Name Basis

There are definitely, right now, some people in your friends and family network who want to read your eBook. You may already have many of these collected on a holiday card list, party, or any event's guest list. Because they know you, they might want to read what you have written just because you wrote it. So give them a chance to decide whether they want to read it by telling them about your book. If they are not personally interested in your topic, they can forward your info to others who are. Many people in your close circle will feel honored to be asked to help you share something which is a true personal accomplishment. Your close circle is automatically expanded if you think of your spouse's close circle, or your child's close circle (their friends' parents, their teachers, or coach.)

Community And Extended Contacts

Broader community contacts can help you find and meet people in your target reader niche. Think about all of the people you interact with and who know you even casually. Think about your associates in business, those you have met in a social setting, people you know in organizations like non-profits, clubs, homeowners' associations, churches, and similar contacts. Then consider which of them would enjoy or benefit from reading your book.

Remember, among this group will be at least one **ideal referrer**. This is someone who regularly comes in contact with your particular niche market, is not a direct competitor of yours, and believes in/endorses what you are doing. For example, if your book is on how to use special exercises to help manage physical challenges from complications of having diabetes, an ideal referrer for you to connect with would be a dietitian who works with diabetics all day every day. The dietitian has a complementary service, not a competing one, and benefits from sharing your book by being a better resource for her clients. Of course the best way to solidify your relationship is to practice mutual referrals whenever possible.

Are you thinking about social media yet? Good! Don't forget your Facebook Friends, LinkedIn contacts and other social media associates. They are part of your community too, so let them know that you have published a book, what's in it, and how some can benefit from it.

The World (Wide Web) Is Your Oyster!

How's your global marketing mindset? There are literally millions of people online who are possible readers for your eBook because, first of all, they are people in the digital world and may already enjoy eBooks and own a Kindle or other e-reader. Later in this book we will detail how to get your eBook into online stores such as Amazon and Barnes & Noble. First let's look at how to put your book in front of your target audience wherever they hang out, not necessarily book shopping at all.

In online discussion groups, for example, you can start a conversation and watch interested people actually market you to each other. These groups may also be called forums, newsgroups, email groups, list serves, or bulletin boards. While overt advertising is frowned upon, you should have the title of your book as part of your signature, and it is not considered bad form to offer free lists, quizzes, and other valuable "bites" to entice people to your site when what you are offering is useful information rather than self-serving hype. Also, think about where you look for answers on the web – Wikipedia? Ask.com? Guru.com? e-How? The keys to success on the web are to get involved, give valuable information, and become known.

There is an interesting story about one gentleman who actually found the material to write his book by participating in an online group. Scott Ringwelski had adopted a Siberian husky from the shelter only to find the dog extremely hard to work with. He began airing his frustrations to subscribers on Sibernet, a group of husky owners. After seventeen tales of woe, he wondered if anyone was reading. Actually, some ten thousand people worldwide were following his stories like a weekly soap opera. He ultimately crafted seventy-eight tales into a book to sell and found that those same group subscribers were some of his best customers.

Other ways to get your book mentioned include submitting articles, writing reviews of other books, writing a blog, writing comments on other peoples' blogs, and giving a copy of your book to bloggers to read and review. Don't overlook your local writers and media people – a local magazine columnist who mentions your topic might be very excited to receive a complimentary copy of your book along with your letter of personal introduction. The connection is easier to make because you are neighbors, so to speak.

Creating Your eBook Marketing Plan: A Critical Step

Good book marketing requires good planning, effective marketing techniques and consistent implementation. The best way to ensure that you will be successful at all three of these is to start with a solid and specific marketing plan for your eBook.

A Successful eBook/Book Marketing Plan is:

- Well-organized, written document that can be referred to and shown to others.

- A plan that takes both your target reader and the eBook marketplace into account.

- A story which starts with some analysis and culminates in describing your eBook from the point of view of the potential reader, e.g., it details benefits that a reader can expect from it rather than simply listing features or chapters of the book.

- A list of the specific things you are going to do to promote the book in the marketplace during a given time. We recommend a six-month, one-year, and three year plan that – is about as far out as planning can make sense in a rapidly-changing environment like the world of eBooks.

- A timeline which includes a decision about each action step, e.g., when does it start, how long will it last, and when will it be completed.

- A plan which has measurable goals so you will know if you have succeeded or need to rethink part of your plan. For example, if you goal is to get a lot of friends for your book's Facebook page, your clearly defined goal might be "500 friends within two years."

Your Book Marketing Plan

A plan is simply a set of successive actions leading to a result. A *marketing plan* is a plan with the capture of your target audience as the intended result.

What's your marketing plan for your dynamic eBook outside of Amazon and your own web site? Follow this book and you will be able to employ your own marketing strategy that will help you effectively reach out to your audience. Consistently getting interested readers to discover your book is the key to success.

Book marketing is not easy but it can be learned and implemented by most anyone as long as they understand its requirements and follow through with what needs to be done. Taking the time to develop a plan, or have a professional create and implement one for you, will save costly mistakes, give your book a fighting chance, and prevent the crushing disappointment of having your launched book sink.

Action Step: Begin Your Marketing Plan

Here is an outline of a typical book marketing plan that we use as a template for the custom marketing plans we develop for our authors. Copy it and then add to it as your plans to market your eBook start to gel in your mind.

Suncoast Digital Press Marketing Plan Outline

Directions: Fill in each section of this outline with a description of what you will do to market your book. Be specific and indicate how the goal will be measured if it is measurable.

Marketing Plan Cover

The Marketing Plan for (your book title)
By: (your name)

Date:

Large photo of your Cover

Section I. Pre-Publication Marketing

My ideal target reader is:

My target reader will get the following benefits from my book:

My target readers read these books, magazines, blogs, etc:

My target readers frequently visit the following web sites:

My target readers read mostly printed or digital material:

I plan on using (fill in the tools you will use and the details of precisely how you plan to use them) to let my target readers know that my eBook is about to be published.

My Full Book Title is:

I have checked each word in my title for search popularity and my results are:

I have created a custom email signature noting my forthcoming book by:

My back cover promotional copy is:

I am asking (fill in names) to endorse my book:

I will publish my book on my web site and at:

I will propose Smart (win-win) Alliances to the following companies and people:

(Detail what you offer and what you want for each.)

Section II. Marketing Blitz Concurrent With Publication

I will send a news release announcing publication to

  Local media list

  National Media List

  The following professional and business organizations:

I will create pages/sites for the following social media. The address for each is:

  Facebook Fan Page

  Facebook Author Page

  Twitter

  LinkedIn

  Pinterest

  Google+

I plan on posting to each of these social media sites every _____(frequency)

My plan to acquire and engage fans on these sites is:

My author web site url is http;// ____ and it will be designed by _____ and will be running by _____

My book web site url is http://_____ and it will be designed by _____ and will be running by ____

My blog will be titled _____.

It will launch on _____

I will register it with the following web sites: ___

The first ten topics I am going to cover in my blog are:

I will write articles on _____ and _____ and _____ and market them on the following article marketing sites:

I will speak on topics _____ and _____ to the following organizations:

My regional author tour will be pitched to the following book stores and book clubs:

My virtual author tour will be pitched to the following blogs and web sites:

I will use _____to maintain my email opt-in list and as a source for email templates.

I will send my first email announcing my book on _____

My video trailer will be created by _____ and be targeted to _____

My video trailer will be _____ long and emphasize the following benefits:

I will advertise my book at:

Section III. Post-Publication Marketing

I will create more traffic at my web sites by:

I will post to my blog every _____

I will become known at additional professional and business portal sites of:

I will plan a second virtual book tour and pitch it to the following:

I will continue to solicit endorsements and reviews from:

I will expand my reputation as a published expert by writing these follow-up books:

1.

2.

3.

I will create the following spin-off products for my book:

1.

2.

I will evaluate each of the steps in my marketing plan by using the following criteria:

[End]

Now that you have your marketing plan outline created, what follows is a discussion of the critical components and the main subheadings for each section of your marketing plan. Use them as catalysts for ideas for your book or eBook.

Smart Authors Engage In Pre-Publication Marketing

Creating and executing a book marketing plan is not something that begins *after* you have written and published your book. It makes good marketing sense to begin to visualize your book out in the marketplace and start working on how that will happen as soon as you have committed to your book idea. Even before you decide on your final book topic and scope you should be thinking about your market — who is going to read and benefit from your book.

Identify Your Target Reader

Since marketing is far more than sales, it involves the whole constellation of features, ideas, and concepts that you will keep in mind when you are writing your book and eventually use to describe your book. The first step in your marketing plan as well as in your writing is to determine who will be the typical reader that you are envisioning for your book. A common mistake is to resist narrowing your target readership to a *niche*, which is simply a group of people with certain key things in common. Think of the red center circle of an archer's target. You want to define and describe the reader inside that bull's eye, the person who can't wait to read your book cover to cover, tell their friends about it and then rush to your web site and email you a raving fan letter about how your book saved their life. Or something like that.

For example, an orthopedic surgeon we know wrote an eBook. Instead of sharing volumes of information like a brain download, this expert wisely decided to write an eBook especially for retired professional athletes. This niche is tightly defined and yet has a population large enough for the book sales he desired. Once you can describe your niche, it is easy to narrow it, or expand it if you are concerned about potential readership size. If your book is about how to use social media to attract new patients and your target market is chiropractors, the positioning could be narrowed to be for newly licensed chiropractors just setting up their first practice who are clueless about marketing. Or, the niche could be expanded to serve health professionals nationwide. Many times a niche expansion will naturally occur after you have served a tightly defined, smaller market and have become known, respected, and have a collection of testimonials. Then you are ready to leverage what you've accomplished to branch out to a larger market.

The more you know about the people you would like to have as readers (and later, as clients) the more able you are to describe and position your book for them. Clearly, this will come in handy when you have the opportunity to put information about your book in front of those who you believe will benefit from reading it. List as many characteristics by which you can identify your ideal reader as you can. Your description should include relevant information such as education level, occupation, geographic locale, and level of affluence. The list should also include as much as you know about what you're target reader reads, listens to, or worries about. The more you can identify the challenges, obstacles or problems your target niche faces, the more successful your book will be.

Be One *In* A Million…. Not One *Of* A Million

A common mistake is to confuse or put off potential customers by being too vague or diverse, like offering a cafeteria of benefits. Today, most people prefer theme restaurants to cafeterias. If they want fish, they go to their favorite seafood restaurant. If they want pizza, they go to their favorite pizza parlor.

This points to why specializing and targeting a niche is so important for you as you write and market your book. Just as it is better to be known as an expert with a specialty, your book will be more successful if it connects powerfully with a niche. If you are a professional photographer, for example, a too-general book idea would be about outdoor photography. A much better idea would be to write a dynamic eBook *Children at the Beach: How to Take Vacation Photos Your Family Will Treasure Forever*.

One entrepreneur considered writing a dynamic eBook about how to write a resume, a cover letter, a book proposal, and a business plan. He considered himself an expert on all of these types of writing, and knew he could save the reader time and costly errors. Instead of one book, as you might guess, he made the wise decision to write several books, each with a narrow focus and bulls eye targeted readership.

Broadcast Your Book's *Benefits* For Your Target Reader On *Their* Radio Station

No matter who your target reader is, did you know that the station they most regularly listen to is *WIIFM*? When evaluating any decision to act, to commit, to read or to purchase your book, for example, he/she is asking, "What's In It For Me?" This is the reason it is necessary for you to clarify the benefits for the reader of your eBook rather than focus on the content or the features within it.

Optimize Your Title

As explained in Chapter IV: *Book Titles: How To Write Powerful, Magnetic Titles And Subtitles*, your title is far more than what you call your book. It is the "handle" that should, ideally, evoke positive thoughts when a potential reader sees it and then compel them to reach for it. Also, a good title is both an evocative description of what the reader should expect to find which is **highly beneficial** to them, *and* a hardworking set of **keywords** that anybody using a search engine and looking for the topic of your book should find. In other words, a good book title both describes what's inside, connects with the reader using *benefit* words, and "invites" search engines to find and present the keywords contained in it. The technical term for such a hard-working title is a *Search Engine Optimized* (SEO) title.

Searching for the right keywords is complex and can be very time-consuming. Fortunately, you have choices. You can do it yourself by using such tools as Google Ad Words to see how often the potential keywords in your title is actually searched for, try other SEO free tools, search Amazon, or you may choose a publisher who offers this service. Refer back to Chapter IV for more explanation about identifying key words and phrases.

Target Reader Locales

Sometimes it makes a lot of sense to use a fishing analogy to describe finding and trying to gently "hook" your reader (all in the context of *Attraction Marketing* rather than using aggressive sales techniques, of course.) When planning a fishing trip, most smart anglers first decide what kind of fish they want to catch. Then they ascertain where those fish are likely to hang out. For example, if you're fishing for bass, you'll find them in fresh water, especially near the bank of a lake with overgrown brush. If you're fishing for tarpon, for example, there is no sense casting at the lake, you will need to go to saltwater. So obviously, to increase your chances of catching a particular kind of fish, you must go fishing in waters where your target fish are likely to be found.

This analogy presents a frame of reference for book marketing as well. Carefully consider the kind of target reader you are trying to attract to your product and cast your bait (title, product, cover shot, key benefits for the potential reader) in the waters where your potential catch already frequents. You want to find the areas where not just a few, but many, like to hang out.

In the case of professionals and entrepreneurs who will be interested in the book that you are writing, your task is to thoroughly research which magazines, professional journals, blogs and web sites he/she is likely to read and find ways to show up in these media. You should also research which professional associations and other business groups your target reader is likely to belong to and present your "attractive marketing lure" to members of those groups by offering to speak to them, or offering to provide free resources to their members.

As you perform the research we have recommended, you may discover that your target ideal reader is not in the business world, but there are still groups, associations and favorite hang-outs you can identify and address in your marketing plan. For example, R.M. has a book idea about a green product which would appeal to the environmentally conscious consumer. One of the places he plans to do a book-signing is a local, but very large, farmers' market. M.J. is writing a book which her research tells her will appeal to well-educated, stay-at-home moms. Where do these women look for books to read? What blogs are most popular in their circle? It is always a good idea to do your homework and figure out the many places where your target reader is already connected. Once you have done this research, go to your market plan and list all that you have found.

The next step, of course, is to develop the right *Attraction Marketing* lure. This will be a combination of your author web site, your book's primary benefits, your personal connections, and most of the techniques that you will find in this chapter.

Before we develop your lure, however, you need to think about three more things: pricing, publishing placement, and smart alliances.

Pricing is a critical part of your marketing plan for your book or dynamic eBook. Even though you may not have completely written or published your book yet, you need to think about price *now*. In the fast-changing eBook publishing environment, pricing is necessarily an integral part of your marketing plan.

Let's first address the electronic versions of your book. What do your target clients or readers expect to pay for a typical eBook? Are you planning to give it away as an inducement for potential clients to buy your other non-book products or services, or are you planning to sell it on popular online bookstores such as Amazon.com or Barnes & Noble.com? If you are going to follow the latter course you need to research the selling price of comparable eBooks. Pricing is as much art as science. There are no hard and fast rules but you probably will not go wrong by emulating what successful authors are charging for analogous books, keeping in mind sometimes the best strategy is to offer it for free.

Remember, there are two strategies possible when positioning your book: the author's strategy which focuses on book sales and therefore pricing is very important, or the marketer's strategy which works on leveraging the book for author benefits, so sales revenue is not paramount – in fact the eBook is often offered as a free download.

Like a tasty sample, many eBooks are utilized as enticing, trust-building introductions to what you most want to attract clients to know about you, and what you provide. Even if you raise the price after a short period, a free opening price can be an excellent launch strategy to build interest and buzz.

Distribution And Where To Publish

Along the same lines, you need to think about where you want to publish your book. Are you going to want to publish it on the big popular bookstores like Amazon.com, Barnes & Noble.com or Apples iTunes? If so, you will not only need to have the various formatting requirements but you should also keep in mind the typical customer on those sites and decide if you are going to appeal to the broader eBook buying public or a smaller business or professional niche. While that is part of what you need to determine as a writer, it should also be part of your marketing plan from the beginning. Again, it is just part of determining an effective "fishing" strategy.

Creating Smart (Win-Win) Alliances

Successful marketing is not a solo enterprise. The more people you can access, the larger your network of contacts online and offline. Simply stated, the larger the size of your marketing network, the more likely you are to increase your readership and business. It is merely a function of percentages. Even if you were to get only a small percentage of prospects to buy your book, the greater the number of prospects you have, the larger the number of readers you will gain for your dynamic eBook. It then follows that the larger the number of people reading your book, the more credible you become. The more credible you become, the more people perceive you as an expert in your field. The more people perceive you as an expert, the more they will want to use your services, and the more successful you will become. A good way to do this is to seek out what Executive Coach Ernest Oreinte calls "smart alliances" in the book, *Smart Alliances*, which he co-authored with Judy Feld.

The key is to think not just like an author as you evaluate possible alliances, but to remember why you are writing your book: most likely it is to attract clients to your business and to enhance your reputation as a go-to expert in your field. Recall what occurred to you when we asked you about your target customer and where that customer can be found.

Now think of businesses that do not directly compete with you who are already marketing to the same potential customers. They are your natural alliance partners, and, as we explained earlier in this chapter, these ideal referrers can become one of your most important relationships.

Contemplate how you can help each other reach and serve the same universe of potential customers, and how those customers would benefit from having both of your services and products. Then contact them and present your ideas. Many, probably most, will say "no thanks," but a few will say "tell me more" or even "Yes." That is your cue to open a dialogue that often results in a true win-win relationship. Once you reach agreement, your mutual task is to implement it. Create a symbiotic relationship by being a good alliance partner and expect the same from your partner.

Regularly monitor whether it not only remains a win-win for you and your alliance partner, but also a win-win-win that includes your customer as well. Start building relationships with potential alliance partners and remember it is wise to first look at how you can assist *them*.

Introducing Your Book to the World

Now let's turn to one of the happiest days in an author's life: the big day that marks the publication of your book! Traditionally, big publishing houses that have chosen to aggressively market a new book in their catalogue will make a big deal about the book's debut, usually termed a "launch." *Book launches* are a good way for you as an independent publisher to drum up excitement, exposure, and sales for a new book.

The date your book finally arrives in stores (on-line or other) marks the culmination of tremendous time and effort. Of course it's a time for celebrating a huge accomplishment! It is also a time to focus on the next big effort…getting your book out to your market. As we've said earlier, if you simply celebrate and then just rest on your laurels at this point, you're likely to be in for a considerable disappointment. You are your own Chief Marketing Officer. And here is a true story: a woman we know recently had her book picked up by a very well-known publishing company, but times have changed – to her surprise, they invested no money at all in promoting her book. She spent thousands of dollars of her own money on book tours and promotions while the publisher takes hefty percentages of every sale. Just in case you had any lingering doubts about self-publishing, it is well to keep this cautionary tale in mind.

PR: Make a Splash Without Much Cash

"PR" is a term that is short for *public relations*. There is a flow of information between you, the author and the *public*, or people in your target market. *Relations* is used to point to the fact that the communication should be back and forth. You are not simply going to broadcast the announcement of your book launch and go to the beach. You are going to draw your potential readers in, and persuade them to respond to your announcement by taking one or more actions. What are some of the actions you want a potential reader to take? You need to incentivize people to go to your web site, purchase your book, post a comment on your blog, read your bio, "Like" you on Facebook, download a sample chapter, read about you on LinkedIn, read the back cover testimonials, and/or tell their friends.

There has never been a better time, because of the World Wide Web, to launch a marketing blitz to get the word out to your target market using methods which are affordable or free. Your PR strategy can be very effective as well as very practical.

Promotion and Publicity

In the context of marketing a book, the goal of PR is to get exposure and generate interest in your book by persuading individuals, opinion gatekeepers like influential bloggers, amateur and professional reviewers and, especially, the media to learn about and form a favorable opinion about your book and you, its author. Within the larger framework of public relations, you will need to develop your action plans for promotion and publicity, which are similar, but there is an important distinction. Basically, *promotion i*s what you, the author can do, and *publicity* is what, if you're good at promoting, you'll get from the media as a result. Both are vital.

Who Cares? Identify Your Best Broadcasters

A major step toward generating free publicity is sending out effective and timely news releases. Many times this type of announcement is called a "press" rather than a "news" release. It's the exact same tool. We are using "news release" because there are so many entities, especially online, who do not consider themselves the press but are constantly disseminating information they deem newsworthy to their readers and followers. Also, what you will be creating and sending is essentially a short news piece. That is why news editors, bloggers, and many other people with the job of keeping their readers abreast of what's new will snatch up a well-written news release to help fill their publications. (It is estimated that fully three-fourths of what you see in print is a result of news releases.) Here are four types of news seekers to target:

- Relevant news and information media, especially local and regional media for a first-time author.

- Local and regional opinion leaders including corporate executives, non-profit executives, and board members, political office holders and anybody you identify as being an influencer or gatekeeper of public opinion constituencies that you want to reach. If you want to spend some money and save time, you can use a professional PR service like PRWeb to send a press release (even one with dynamic elements) to either a regional or national media list.

- Professional and business group leaders and members (especially regional or local but could also be national if your book is narrow and cast to their particular interests) who are likely to be interested in, or profit from, the subject matter of your book.

- Bloggers and other online gatekeepers who write about your book topic.

Next, make a list for each PR category that includes a good contact person, a "snail mail" address, and an email address.

Then write an appropriate pitch to each, and compose an email news release about the publication of your book. If you are not conversant with how to write a news/press release, you can go to PRWeb.com and download the free *Guide to Writing Great Online Press Releases*. For regional or local media, be sure to emphasize your local connection since newspapers and radio and TV stations like to talk about their own community members whenever possible. For professional associations or relevant opinion leaders, be sure to customize your release so you mention what is likely to interest them. A canned release addressed to a general audience is easily spotted and is likely to be taken less seriously than a custom-targeted message.

A news release is *not* a sales document. Stick to the *who*, *what*, *when* and *how* of your pitch for publicity, and avoid sales hype at all costs. Reporters and media contacts are a savvy bunch and can see through "pseudo news" and thinly disguised marketing pitches with ease. Both of these are likely to launch your news release on a short trip to the trash.

Dynamic (multimedia) news releases get attention and we recommend them. If you have video shooting and editing skills or are willing to hire a videographer to do it for you, including a short but very professional video about your book is a nice touch. Like the dynamic elements in your eBook, this will help you make an outstanding impression which sets you apart. In fact, you may already have an excellent video clip to use if you created any video elements for your eBook.

We also recommend creating a "one sheet" (a one or two-sided fact sheet about your book that contains a cover image, a table of contents, and some very basic and low-key promotional copy that emphasizes who is the ideal reader and what benefits they can expect) and including it as an attachment to your news release.

Social Media Marketing

According to the online *Wikipedia* site, Social Media Marketing refers to the process of gaining attention or web site traffic through social media sites. Popular examples of social media sites include Facebook, LinkedIn, Twitter, Google+ and Pinterest.

Social media marketing programs center on the creation of content that attracts attention and encourages readers to share it with their social networks. A company's message spreads from user to user and presumably resonates because it appears to come from a trusted, third-party source, as opposed to the brand or company itself. It is the 21st century epitome of *Attraction Marketing* which leverages word-of-mouth market penetration vs. advertising and promotion paid for by a company.

Social media has become a platform that is easily accessible to anyone with Internet access. Increased communication for organizations fosters brand awareness and, often, improved customer service. Additionally, social media serves as a relatively inexpensive platform for organizations to implement marketing campaigns. In fact, it makes sense to create a strong social media presence even before you publish your book since you can use social media to attract friends and followers for you as an author and for your book project. You can build excitement among your network, and your network's network, in anticipation of your book launch.

The process of becoming a social media presence is fairly simple. First, you create your social media pages (actually mini Internet sites) and make them look both attractive and professional. Don't forget to fill out your profile as completely as you can so that your visitors have some background about you or your business. This is your chance to make your good first impression, so make the effort to create a professional and inviting introduction.

Next, when you are satisfied with how your social media pages look, it's time to tell the world about them. Send emails to your business and social contacts, put the URL of your pages in your email signature, and generally tell folks that your pages exist.

Start to use the social resources that you have created. A few minutes each day, if you are consistent, will build your network and online relationships more quickly than you might imagine. As you post, the way to build a good reputation for you and your book is to become a trusted source of good ideas and useful information. Think attraction or magnetic marketing, not hype and hard sell, and you'll find yourself on the right track.

As a good start, authors should create (or hire someone to create) the following social media pages or sites:

- **Facebook Fan Page**. (www.Facebook .com) This site allows you, for free, to provide detailed descriptions, testimonials, images, photos, videos and messages to attract and build interest for your book. When you publish a book, you are creating a business with that book, whether you intend to sell it or give it away as a marketing tool for your principal business. For that reason alone, your book deserves its own Facebook Fan Page. More than three quarters of U.S. businesses have a Facebook presence and your book should too.

  Once you have created your Facebook Fan Page, be sure to let your whole network know about it and ask them to "like" it. (This really helps your efforts to become prominent in Internet search results.) Then, as people become fans and comment, be sure to engage them in a dialogue and provide tips and ideas about the subject of the book.

- **Twitter** (www.twitter.com) encourages individuals to pay attention to a message by keeping it very brief. You can "message" your followers with up to 140 characters. Create your twitter page and use it to post bits of information and ideas about the subject of your book. You can also use Twitter's search capability to find Twitter users, called "tweeters," who share your interests, and start to follow them. They will be notified that you are following them and some will follow you in return, thereby growing your network. The interactions, though brief, serve to build brand loyalty and can lead to a tremendous increase in awareness for your book and your business.

- **LinkedIn** (www.LinkedIn.com) is a smart place to be for business and professional people. Among its 100 million-plus members are a *Who's Who* in the business and professional world, as well as a huge pool of potential readers for your book, no matter what the subject. Take care in filling out your LinkedIn profile so that it is thorough, professional, has a good photo of you, and highlights the book(s) you have written or are writing.

As a member, you can use "Company Pages" similar to Facebook pages to create an area especially to promote your business and your book, in particular. You are creating an invaluable opportunity to promote your book and to interact with your potential readers and customers.

LinkedIn has many "Groups" too. Search for the ones that interest you and join them. You want to find the best "fishing holes" like we explained earlier, so that your efforts are efficient and effective. We recommend that you introduce yourself and start to post useful tips and ideas as soon as you get the hang of the group's culture.

- **Pinterest** (www.pinterest.com) is a relatively new but phenomenally fast-growing social medium that allows members to "pin" things to an online bulletin board. It is very graphically-oriented so be sure to include your book cover and post relevant visuals with your recommendations and tips. Again, it's great opportunity to become known at a glance by many, many potential readers just by investing a little time.
  Google+ (https://plus.google.com/) is, in many ways, a rival of Facebook. Since it has the marketing might of the Google juggernaut behind it, it is a must-use site.

- **YouTube** is where people go to view video clips. In fact, a lot of people. Over 800 million unique users visit the site each month. 72 hours of video are uploaded every minute. In 2011, YouTube had more than 1 trillion views, or around 140 views for every person on Earth. Millions of subscriptions happen each day. Subscriptions allow you to connect with someone you're interested in – like an author you saw on Pinterest – and keep up with their activity on the site. There are different options to utilize this site for promoting your book including ads and sponsoring videos. You can easily set up your own YouTube "Channel" – check this one out:

Your Internet Presence

The World Wide Web is the biggest thing to hit marketing since the invention of the printing press. Savvy book marketers take advantage of its tremendous reach and impact by using the following tools (in conjunction with social media.)

Blogs

A blog is short for web log. It is a discussion or information site, or pages on your web site that you write and make public. The usual subject (and one we highly recommend) is the subject that you cover in your book – plus others that you know as an expert in your field. You should create and contribute to your blog as part of your marketing blitz for your new book, and for any others you may have published.

While some write blogs that resemble streams of consciousness or personal diaries, we discourage that for authors of business and professional books. Your credibility as an expert published author will be enhanced if you stick to business topics and offer information, news and insights to your readers that are useful, topical and timely to those who you think would benefit from reading your book or eBook. Do not take this to mean you should be formal, dry or boring. The most popular bloggers have personality as well as something of value to say.

Your blog posts do not have to be lengthy or complex. If you write just a few paragraphs and keep them interesting, grammatically correct, and useful to your readers, your blog will be an attractive but subtle advertisement for you and your endeavors as an author. Be sure the blog title and entry contain as many of your SEO key words as possible.

You should update your blog regularly, *at least* a couple of times a month or more often if you have time. When you do update your blog with a new entry, be sure to post about it on your social media sites and invite people to read it.

It is not good enough just to upload your blog. With the web as vast as it is, you have to market it just as you have to market your book or eBook. According to the marketing experts at Hubspot.com, there are three critical steps in blog marketing:

1) You have to attract brand new readers and traffic to your blog by publicizing it.

2) Next, you should strive to convert visitors into subscribers who stick around and keep coming back.

186

3) Once you accomplish the first two, it is time to identify your true evangelists from your networks of subscribers and encourage them to share your content and make your ideas (and your book) even more viral.

Article Marketing

Writing and publishing articles is another good way to market your book. Basically, it is taking articles you write (often excerpts or amplifications of content from your own book) and sending them to other sites for people to discover and use. Two that we find useful are Ezinearticles.com, and IdeaMarketers.com, but there are many others as well. When you join those sites and upload your articles, you can set the permissions parameters for people to download and use them. We recommend that you allow free copying and use as long as you get full attribution and a link to your book's web site so that your reputation as an author spreads.

We also recommend that you repurpose your articles by posting them (or excerpts of them) to your blog and mention that they are available in you social media posts.

A good form of article marketing is offering to be a contributor to other blogs. You can find relevant blogs by searching for topics in your field at http://technorati.com, http://networkedblogs.com, http://blogarama.com and http://bloghub.com.

Speeches

Speaking to groups of any size is one of the best ways an author can build his/her *platform.* This is a commonly used term which refers to building and communicating to your following – people who already have an experience of you (the author) and want more (evidenced by such things as they follow you on Twitter, read your blog, and/or refer others to you.) Fortunately, by this point, a lot of your platform-building work has already been accomplished simply by building your expertise, credibility, and previous marketing efforts such as your web site and social media presence.

The speaker's podium is a fantastic author's marketing tool. It is a good idea to try to schedule as many talks as you can as your book is published (or before!) so that you can tell your audiences about it. One of the keys to all your marketing is for you to be able to communicate effectively and positively about your topic/your book.   You may be more comfortable thinking about making a "presentation' rather than a speech, given the common fear of public speaking. You can choose the theme of your presentation (to educate, to entertain, to persuade, etc.) based on what you are most comfortable with, as well as what is appropriate for a particular audience.

You can polish your presentation and speaking skills by joining Toastmaster's International and attending club meetings in your area (listed on Toastmasters.org) Even if you know you would never give formal speeches or address large crowds, you can master this area of communication so you are comfortable and confident talking about your book or anything else in any situation.

Civic organizations like Rotary, Kiwanis and Lions chapters are always looking for good speakers. So are local business networking groups and a wide variety of clubs and organizations.

Make a list of organizations you would like to speak to and contact their speaker chairs. You can locate some in the calendar listings in your local newspaper or its web site, search for them online, check your local Chamber of Commerce, and ask friends and colleagues.

Once you have your list, contact the speaker chairs by email or phone. Tell them who you are, including that you are the author of a book, and that you want to speak to their group. Be sure to give your talk a title (preferably one that is intriguing like *Ten Things You Need To Know About [My Book Topic]* and send them the one-sheet you created. To increase your chances of being selected by the program chairperson, create several different titles which all relate to your topic so they have a choice. If they ask you if you have a fee for speaking, you should say that there is no fee for community minded groups like theirs. Your pay is the valuable exposure you will get. With more experience, however, you may find you enjoy speaking, giving seminars, or workshops which would be appropriate to charge a fee for presenting.

When you speak to the group, make your talk long on information and short on sales. In your pre-written speaker introduction, be sure and mention the book by name, and possibly what inspired you to write it, and if it has gotten any rave reviews or media attention. Then the person introducing you as the presenter or speaker does the "selling" so you don't have to. Again, think *Attraction Marketing* rather than sales hype. In most cases you can expect to be allowed to set up a table in the back of the room with a display and your books for sale. Often it works out that you can stay after the presentation, sell and sign books. (By the way, even eBooks can be sold at live events by providing the digital version on a thumb drive.) But never make your audience think that you are standing in front of them primarily to sell your book. You are there to share valuable information as an expert, not as a book vendor.

Plan ahead to capture and leverage the moment. If you can get a good photograph of you speaking to a group, it is likely you can obtain their permission and send the photo out along with a press release about your presentation. If you can get video, you can use it on your web site, in a press release, in your speaker's resume, or for other opportunities for more visibility.

Regional Author Tours

The old fashioned book tour is not dead yet. It can be a very useful tool for your publication marketing salvo. Unlike virtual online author tours, you appear in person to discuss your book with interested readers and potential readers. Contact area bookstores, book clubs, and similar organizations and offer to talk about your new book.

If it is only an eBook, you will not have physical copies to autograph but you can download copies to USB flash memory drives and sell them if you wish. These small devices (which we discussed in Chapter VII) can be pre-loaded with your eBook, articles, company information, video book trailer, testimonials—

and can be custom-stamped with your name, book name, or company logo.

Unfortunately, there are not many bookstores left today, so it might be difficult to find a lot of venues for your book tour, but it is worth the effort to try to locate and speak at as many book sales outlets (whether traditional bookstores or not) as possible. Public libraries could be receptive as well. Depending on your topic, it may make sense to offer to do book-signings at other public events such as festivals, grand openings, hobby gatherings or career fairs. You may not achieve celebrity status at first and sign hundreds of books at each crowded appearance, but your success usually builds with practice and publicity.

At a minimum, consider having one live event – a launch party! Invite everyone you know, open the community invitation as widely as you can accommodate guests, and graciously host a one-themed celebration: your book's debut. Send a press release about it to local media, and blast news about it far and wide on social media and everywhere else you can.

Virtual Author Tours

A great Internet-age marketing tool for books and eBooks is a virtual book tour. They are starting to become common, and we recommend them highly. Instead of showing up physically at the fast-disappearing venue of a book store, you offer to talk about your book at author portal websites, blogs, relevant business and professional organizations, and any place on the web where their visitors are your readers.

It can be productive to be interviewed for blog talk radio, but also you can target individual bloggers. Search for possible blogs and ask if they would be interested in featuring you during your tour. Make it a win-win by offering to talk about them in your blog and sending them a complimentary copy of your book. Once they accept, follow the rules of *Attraction Marketing*. Such tours are time consuming to organize but can be very productive because you and your book can receive such wide exposure. You never know where your fans may reside!

Email

Email is still an important marketing tool for any author to promote a newly published book. Be sure and add your eBook title and a link to your signature file in your email program. Also, online companies like Constant Contact and MailChimp offer attractive templates and will maintain your email lists for a fairly nominal monthly fee. Using the opt-in principle of list building (asking people if they want to be on your list, often in return for a free report) can help you build a list quickly. Your initial email to the people on your list should be to thank them for signing up and letting them know that that you have published your book, a little bit about it, and where they can get it. Again, the emphasis should be on useful information for the reader rather than a thinly disguised sales pitch.

Another fast-growing trend is to use video in your email and social media marketing strategy. They increase both interest and click-through rates. If your videos are very short, you can insert them in an email or social media post and not take up too much bandwidth. If they are longer, it makes sense to upload them to video sites like YouTube or Vimeo and link to them so you use their bandwidth and your email or post does not take too long to load, or fail because your video file is too large to email.

Book Video Trailer

A book trailer is analogous to the promotional previews called "trailers" that Hollywood creates for its new releases and is another great marketing tool for authors. If you are not adept at videography and video editing, you should have a professional create your trailer for you. Something amateurish will not inspire confidence in you as an author or the content of your book.

Your trailer does not have to be long or resemble typical "Hollywood Hype" trailers, but it should have fully professional production values and tell potential readers about the benefits of reading your book. One good idea is to include an interview with you, the author. Once you have your trailer, you can make it part of your virtual book tour, your promotional emails, social media, put it on your book and business web sites, send it with news releases, and use it wherever you can.

The most advanced version of a book trailer is actually a scripted short film with actors recreating a scene or scenes from your book. While usually for a novel, you can consider this exciting and cutting edge marketing idea for any book, even a nonfiction business book. If you are an attorney, why not create a little courtroom drama, or show yourself at your best while working with your target market?

There are many benefits to producing a trailer including that video "views" on your web site will improve your site's SEO. YouTube is the largest video host currently, with over one billion unique visitors each month. Since video communication is exploding, you should keep up with developments and the rapidly-growing number of video hosting sites so you are always using the most popular and effective media for your book trailer.

Targeted Display or Web Advertising

Advertising targeted to reach your intended book audience in certain highly-targeted print publications or web sites can be a useful adjunct to a business book launch if you have the budget and if you can locate professional or business association web sites, meeting or event program books, or similar niche places to promote your book.

The main advantage of this kind of advertising when compared to advertising in media that appeals to a general audience, is that it is very targeted. If you pick the right association or conference program, most of those who view your display advertisement should be in your target market. The main disadvantage of display and web advertising is that they are often quite pricey. The advertising cost includes not only the cost of printing and distribution plus a reasonable profit much the way magazines and newspapers price their ads, but also must help cover the cost of the meeting, or running the association. Consequently, such ads can be quite expensive on a cost per thousand basis. For that reason, carefully consider the return on investment and use them judiciously.

As for other advertising, we don't recommend purchasing display advertising in mass circulation newspapers or magazines or large portal websites for business books because their vast audiences contain only a small portion of your target market and the costs are usually prohibitive on a cost-per-useful-impression basis.

Keep The Marketing Engine Stoked: It Takes Time To Build An Empire

A caveat is in order here. Time is almost always a factor in marketing. Unless you have a huge budget and a lot of circumstances align for you serendipitously (including many you have no control over such as the economy, current events, and similar unpredictable factors that affect buying habits) your marketing will not produce instant results. All marketing is a long-term process and *Attraction Marketing* in particular takes time to build great results, although in the long run it is probably more effective than any other type of marketing for an author.

Even though your marketing blitz upon publication is over, your marketing must continue. If you have used the tools we have discussed, it is likely that you have announced the existence of your new book and, by implication, your credibility as an expert author to a large number of people. Now you need to engage them and make them fans of what you do.

You must keep news of your book fresh in order to reach the multitude of people who missed your original launch and marketing blitz, and to hold the interest of people who have opted in to your list. The way this is accomplished is by organizing all the marketing strategy elements you have created into a system. Your ongoing book marketing system will include what actions to take, how to take them, and the frequency of performing those tasks. For example, part of your system could be to write three blog entries every Monday and post one to your web site and Facebook every Monday, Wednesday and Friday.

Many authors ask how long do you need to market your book? The short answer is that marketing is worthwhile for as long as you have it available for sale or as a free download. The two authors of this book continue to get sales of both print and digital versions of books they wrote as many as ten years ago. True, sales peaked soon after publication and then declined but they have far from disappeared. Every time we market them, we make sales because the topics (business writing, for example) continue to be relevant. Even when we publish new editions and eBooks on new topics, the original books will still exist and will still be worth reading.

Here are some of the best ways to build long-term engagement with your new audience.

- Keep publishing your blog and fill it with great tips about your subject.

- Put "author of XYZ" on your business cards, your web site, email signature, any professional advertising you might do, and all marketing collateral pieces you produce for your business.

- Have business cards printed for your book. Put the title, your name, your cover, a significant endorsement (e.g., "Must reading for anybody who wants to understand how to deal with pain"— Jane Jones, M.D.) and where to get your book. Hand these cards out wherever you speak or appear professionally, especially at opportunities with your target readers.

- Set a goal and schedule yourself regularly to speak to groups.

- Search the web for targeted portal web sites that specialize in the subject matter of your book and appeal to your target market. Once you have found them, join them if membership is offered and get to know their culture and style. Once you are familiar with them, offer to be a contributor. After all, you are now a published expert author so you are qualified.

- Start your own social media groups (especially on LinkedIn and Facebook) and engage regularly with them. As you engage, don't be formal or stiff. You can let your personality come through while still being businesslike.

- Whenever you do something significant such as speaking to a group, winning an award or recognition, or passing a sales milestone for your book, send a news release about it and put the release on the news page on your book web site. (You do have a news page on your book and author web sites, don't you?)

- Other good topics for news releases are surveys you conduct, media appearances you make, or anything that is news about you or your book.

  Become a media personality by pitching your expertise in your subject and your willingness to act as a commentator or analyst to reporters, radio and TV station news directors and Internet news sites and Internet radio sites which you can find at http://alltalkradio.net, and http://blogtalkradio.com.

- Ask your friends and network of contacts to review your book and post their review to Amazon.com and any place where your book is offered or where reviews are posted. A handy list of review sites can be found at http://publishing.about.com/cs/reviews1/

  Once you have favorable reviews and testimonials, ask permission from your reviewers and fans to put them on your web site. Audio or video versions are great too.

- Plan and conduct another virtual book tour. Re-pitch all the sites you requested as "tour stops" because many that initially said no might be ready to say yes since your marketing has percolated around the region and the Internet.

It's Okay To Admit You Have Your Next Book Already In Mind

If you really want to extend your reputation as an author and go-to expert in your field, don't stop publishing. It is even more impressive to be the author of a coordinated series of books on your chosen topic than to be the author of just one. As you finish your first book, you may want to plan the sequels to it. After all, as a published author you have learned a lot about writing and marketing your book and have broadened your base of contacts measurably. It will be far easier to get the attention of the gatekeepers for your target market if you can tell them that you are the author of XYZ book and now you are publishing another book in the same field.

Being the author of more than one book in a given field is also an excellent marketing tool for your business. The more books you have in the marketplace, the greater are the chances that one or more of them will be discovered by potential clients.

The key to sustained success as an author is planning. You've got more to say…plan your next book book now and integrate it into a lifelong writing strategy. A good first step is to recall your original book idea germination process and review all the good ideas you had for books that you set aside. Most will still make sense so it is time to pick them up again and refine them by asking the same set of clarifying questions you used before.

You probably also several book reviews to look at, and feedback and comments from readers. It's time to go over those and glean the good ideas and requests about what people would have liked to have seen in your book.

As part of your planning process, remember that your book can be a springboard to other products and programs as well. Once you have established yourself as a published expert in your field, you can use the same research and information to launch your own information products on the topic of your book. You can create and sell audio and video courses, offer seminars and workshops in person or as webinars, become a professional platform speaker who gets paid to talk about your subject, and you could even become a consultant or coach in your field. You may be surprised how many ways you can leverage your book using companion and alternate formats. Jay Conrad Levinson once answered an interview question about how much he made from his first *Guerilla Marketing* book by saying "10 million dollars." He explained that he made $35,000 in book revenue, and $9,965,000 from all the spin-off information products.

Being a published author clearly and significantly improves your position in the market no matter how you want to expand your business, your brand, or your outreach. With your book and the many additional opportunities to re-purpose and leverage it, you and your message are going to reach an exponentially greater number of people than ever before. While academics often talk with trepidation about the "publish or perish" culture of modern higher education that forces them to write with few benefits for them personally other than keeping their jobs, book authors are in much less of a writing pressure cooker. For us, it's "publish and flourish."

Key Distinctions For This Chapter

Claiming Your New Status Now vs. Waiting To Be Discovered   You are soon to become a published author and as you begin to think that way, and speak that way, you will naturally find many opportunities to share this good news with the world. Even before you finish your book you should claim your new status by announcing that you are the "author of the forthcoming book, _____." Integrate your news in your introductions, on-line profiles and conversations.

Attraction Marketing vs. Hard-Sell or Seduction   People do not respond in a positive way to being arm-twisted or manipulated; they run away. The *Attraction Marketing* approach acts like a magnet to attract potential customers your way. Simply communicate the customer benefits so effectively that people get it, and your book will attract plenty of readers. Use this approach to develop and implement a comprehensive marketing plan.

Summary

Books do not sell themselves. You must have, and implement, a marketing plan to succeed. In today's crowded book and eBook marketplace, just "putting a book out there" will not create many sales or downloads, if any. Marketing before publication, simultaneously with publication, and for the long haul after publication, is truly the key to making your book a success. Use this "Cheat Sheet" to help you save a lot of time, and not miss anything really important.

Suncoast Digital Press Self-Publishing Marketing Cheat Sheet

Use this checklist to get ready to market your book or eBook.

Pre-Publication Marketing: Introduction To Your Target Reader

☐ Create a One-Sheet with reader benefits.

☐ Choose an SEO-verified title.

☐ Add "author of the forthcoming book "_____" to your email signature and other   personal profiles.

☐ Make market-driven decisions about your book format(s) and distribution channels.

☐ Register a domain name for your author and book web sites.

☐ Create a cover with impact.

☐ Design a back cover and secure promotional endorsements for it.

Marketing Concurrent With Publication

☐ Create a Facebook Fan Page for your book and ask for "Likes."

☐ Ask for reviews.

☐ Open your Twitter account.

☐ Start tweeting when you acquire followers.

☐ Open a Google+ account and use and promote it.

☐ Open a Pinterest account and use and promote it.

☐ Design and run your book or author web sites.

☐ Determine need for possible display advertising in highly targeted publications.

☐ Create your own Facebook and LinkedIn groups.

☐ Create a video book trailer.

☐ Plan and book a regional book tour.

☐ Plan and book a virtual book tour.

Post-Publication Marketing

☐ Post to your blog monthly.

☐ Inform the media that you are available for expert appearances.

☐ Continue your speaking engagements.

☐ Introduce yourself as an expert to bloggers, and business and industry portal web sites.

☐ Plan and implement another virtual book tour.

☐ Plan your next eBooks and spin-off products.

Chapter XII

Tracking Success

Readers, Sales and Revenue & Measuring Market Response

Tracking Success

Publishing and promoting a book is serious business indeed. You have devoted countless hours to your book and the truism that *time is money* certainly applies. If you have written your book for business purposes, this is doubly true. Your book project should be approached like any other commercial venture, whether it is a stand-alone book developed as a product, or a marketing and promotional tool for your professional practice or a business.

Because your book is such a valuable professional tool, it makes sense to treat it as a business unto itself by setting up and regularly updating sales and revenue tracking mechanisms. Even if your book is not offered for a fee, you need to know how many people are downloading it to read so you can track how well various marketing strategies are working. Knowing which sources attract the most readers allows you to make appropriate decisions to continually increase your results.

What Is Book Tracking?

Even before a book is published, and especially as soon as a book is published, whether it is a print book, an eBook or a dynamic eBook, the first thing most authors do is launch a sustained marketing blitz. (The various methods, means, venues and all you need to know about "blitzing" your book are covered in Chapter XI on marketing.)

When you have launched and stayed with your marketing blitz for a while, you should start to see interest building in your book. Fortunately, a great deal of that interest is measurable. Tracking is a process for identifying some key metrics that show how your marketing efforts are affecting the desired goals for your book. By setting up a system of processes, you will be able to measure the effectiveness of each marketing effort objectively, and have a record of how they change over time.

Why Track?

The reason tracking is important is that **information is critical to market planning** and execution. The more you know about how well you are meeting your goals as an author, the more able you will be to fine tune your efforts and stay on course as your book marketing evolves. In short, knowing your key indicators enables you to make better decisions.

Just as well-run businesses track their performance in the marketplace so they know what is going on with their products, your tracked information will help evaluate how changes affect your intended goals. Then you will be able to better respond to these changes and either sustain, accelerate, or modify your marketing tactics to bring about your desired ends.

"Measurement is the first step that leads to control and eventually to improvement. If you can't measure something, you can't understand it. If you can't understand it, you can't control it. If you can't control it, you can't improve it."

H. James Harrington, Ph.D.
(Former head of IBM Quality Research Center)

While there are many valid reasons to track your book's progress in the marketplace, there are four main book goals that nearly every author should track so he or she can evaluate marketplace results and trends. Tracking your book's progress toward realizing these goals will not only give you a barometer of what is happening but also what may be possible. You will have more clarity on many important factors as you evaluate opportunities, and you can more easily decide how to allocate your time and resources.

Having a book means more than just having a book; it means having a stronger platform, and many aspects of one's professional and personal life can be affected. You should have goals so you can be mindful about these outcomes. As a nonfiction author, these examples of goals illustrate important areas which you can choose to focus on and track. Again, here are examples but you need to clearly state your own goals.

1. **Building your business** by writing about your area of expertise and mentioning your company and/or its products and having others mention them as they discuss your book.

2. **Increasing traffic to your web site or social media pages** and thereby making it more likely that some of these visitors will buy your book, hire you, or at least *hear* you.

3. **Building your professional reputation** through establishing credibility as a published expert, receiving media attention, peer recognition, and public speaking.

4. **Gaining a passive income stream** through royalties and direct book sales.

If your results turn out as you envisioned, then great – keep doing what you're doing and enjoy your rewards. If some parts of your marketing blitz are working *better* than anticipated, then you should accelerate those that are succeeding and lessen your emphasis on what does not seem to be working. If you see a trend emerging that was not part of your original plan, it might be a good sign that you should embrace that and track it more intensely. If not much is happening anywhere after a 60 days, you will be able to analyze your efforts more easily because you have been tracking them. Then you can make changes and continue tracking results. Like an expert sailor, you can use this process of course correction to evolve your marketing plan and navigate to your destination of success.

Another use of the data you collect includes testing various new marketing initiatives against each of your main goals. If you have been promoting a particular goal using an email campaign, for example, you might also try promoting by Twitter and blog posts and compare the results.

What To Track

If you wish to track metrics for the general goals enumerated above as well as other indices, you need to know which indicators you should track. While they vary somewhat with each marketplace and the specific target reader you have in mind for your book, there are some recurring items that almost every author should track.

Here are a few examples of key indicators and a short summary of what they tell you:

- **Sales (or downloads if your book is free**.) This is a critical raw measure of your book's performance in the marketplace. If you are selling your book on Amazon.com, Barnes & Noble's Nook eBook store, Apple iTunes, your own web site and anywhere else you have listed them for sale, you should check each one regularly, or get reports automatically sent to your email. The same goes for sites where you offer free downloads.

- **Blog readership**. How many people are reading your blog once you mention your book's publication in it is an important measure of interest in your message. Number of **comments** on your blog is also a measurable indicator of high interest, which is a good goal. (Reader interest, plus opportunity to acquire, equals sales.)

- **Growth of your opt-in email list.** The more people you have on your list, the more business opportunities available even if your response percentages remain flat. Your list may be growing as a result of new subscribers to your newsletter, or number of people who give their contact information in exchange for your free eBook, a free chapter, or a related special report. Have your list set up so it is automatically updated in real time so you can see the current size of the list at any time.

- **Traffic at your book and/or author web sites**. Use Google analytics to track not just the number of visitors but how many page views they saw, how many were new visitors, and how long they stayed on the web sites.

- **Traffic and activity at your book's social media sites**. Since social media are becoming increasingly important as marketing channels, you need to track visits, "likes", "follows" and other forms of engagement (including Facebook page posts, re-tweets and similar indices.) At a minimum, every author should have a LinkedIn Profile, Twitter account, a Facebook Fan Page and a Google+ page. Pinterest is also growing in influence and there are many other social media that come and go. Since it is almost impossible to predict which one(s) will get "hot", our best advice is to try any which capture your attention, have generated buzz in your target market, or that you see your competitors using. Then track the results to determine if they are worth maintaining.

Another thing to track is your growing reputation as a published author and expert in your field. This important variable is not as tangible as the indices above and therefore more difficult to measure. Nevertheless, here are four indirect indicators that are worth tracking because of the insights they provide.

- **Business web site traffic trends**. Although most established business web sites have flows of traffic from many sources including search engines, existing customers, organizations they participate in, and other similar sources, traffic coming from your book-specific web site, your author website and your book-specific social media sites are traceable and can show increased interest in you/your business generated by your book.

- **Increase in potential client or customer inquiries not directly attributed to other non-book-oriented marketing initiatives**. If you have an effective mechanism in your business to track all of your marketing initiatives and programs, and there is a rise in customer inquiries not directly related to any of them, this is good indirect evidence that your book is working to enhance your professional stature.

- **Invitations to participate in professional and business events and presentations.** As you get invited to sit on panels, be a guest speaker, or otherwise participate in professional organizations and business events, the more evidence mounts that you are becoming an in-demand, go-to authority and that your book is working. Track those incoming invitations and also the percentage of your outgoing queries about opportunities which result in public appearances for you.

- **Media inquiries about your book or you as an author**. If the media calls to ask your opinion on things, to interview you, or to inquire about your book, that is an excellent, trackable sign that your reputation as an author is taking hold. Also, when you contact the media with a press release, article or book review, you can track their responses. More publicity means stronger positioning in the marketplace, leading to more credibility and ability to connect with your target readers.

How To Track

The actual process of tracking in not complicated. It simply takes some organization at the beginning and a willingness to invest a little time to achieve useful results. If you approach it this way, your valuable information return on your time investment will be well worth the effort.

Step One is to list and review your goals. Review your work in previous chapters in this book. Why did you write your book? Consider whether building your business, increasing traffic to your web site or social media pages, building your professional reputation and/or gaining a passive income stream are of key importance. Don't stop at your major goals, though. List other possible goals that make sense to you because tracking these also will provide you with measures to evaluate what is working with your book in direct sales or downloads or with indirect benefits. Also, tracking often leads to discovering unanticipated outcomes and trends.

Step Two is to prioritize your goals for tracking efficiency. While you can track just about anything, to do so would take an inordinate amount of time with dubious return on investment. The bulk of your tracking effort should be focused on your most compelling goals. Track your top four or five goals, including several variables to evaluate, and review the results at least once a month. Analyzing this information (**key indicators**) helps you see at a glance what is going on with your book, and empowers your decision-making. Track the rest of your goals to review quarterly and include only a few indices for each.

Step Three is to determine measures to track within each main and subsidiary goal. Here are some key indicators that make sense to track for the main goals we have discussed:

Goal: Building Your Business

Key Indicators:

Orders for books

Free book downloads or related bonus items (e.g., from your company web site)

Conversions and upselling

Source of leads (ask new prospects or customers where they heard about you)

Referrals

Google alerts for mentions of you, your business and your book

Goal: Increasing traffic to your web site or social media pages

Key Indicators:

Google analytics - hits on pages, entry/exit pages, each page dwell time

How many sites link to yours:
http://www.wholinks2me.com/

Goal: Building your professional reputation

Key Indicators:

Speaking engagements; invitations to sit on panels of professional associations

Promotion or election to Officer position

Referrals from other professionals as well as customers

Citations of your book(s) by other professionals

Number of people who contact you (usually via email) after reading about you or reading a column or article you wrote.

Number of publications accepting your articles or other contributions

Goal: Gaining a passive income stream

Key Indicators:

Revenue/royalties at every bookstore and your own website

Orders for multiple books, such as by teachers or consultants

Example of a secondary goal: Obtain reviews of your book on Amazon and other online bookstores

Key Indicator: Number of reviews and ratings if applicable

Step Four is to set up a tracking system using software. One application widely used is an Excel® spreadsheet, but you can use a table in your word processor, or database software, accounting software, or any other tool that you have and are comfortable using. There is no need to invest in expensive new programs or learn how to use complex databases since your goal is simply to record relevant numbers so you can look at trends over time. You will find that these key indicators will be invaluable in your decision-making.

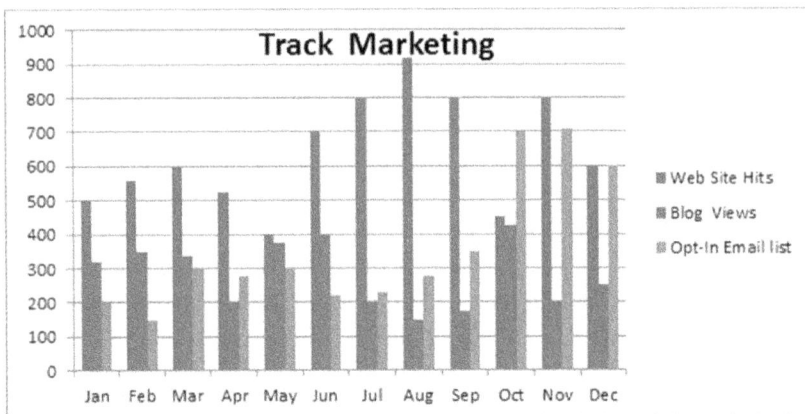
Track Marketing

Legend: Web Site Hits, Blog Views, Opt-In Email list

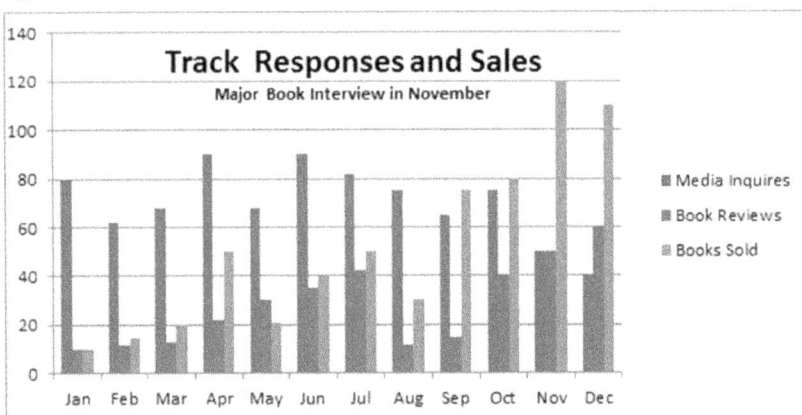
Track Responses and Sales
Major Book Interview in November

Legend: Media Inquires, Book Reviews, Books Sold

Step Five is to think about your own network of resources, and also to go online to research where you can find data for each variable you are tracking on your list. Note these sources and set up a system which lays out the step-by-step procedures and frequencies you will use to update and maintain your tracking. Having a system will make it efficient and simple for you, on a regular basis, to enter the numbers you find into your spreadsheet or other software.

Step Six is to examine your data, your key indicators, for trends over time and respond to them. You must use your system for maintaining the statistics you are tracking as well as set a regularly scheduled time to review and analyze the results.

Sustaining Your Tracking

Don't judge your tracking statistics too quickly. Time is almost always a factor in marketing. Good marketing is a long-term process. As discussed in Chapter XI, remember that *Attraction Marketing* takes time to build great results, although in the long run it is probably more effective than any other type of marketing for an author. Give your book time to percolate the marketplace and work its potential magic for you. While you may want to review your results frequently, especially soon after your book launch, it is best to wait 60-90 days to analyze them for decision-making purposes.

Key Distinctions For This Chapter

Goal Setting vs. Goal Achievement   Goal-setting is integral to planning but can be challenging when there is no past performance to inform you. Once you identify key indicators and track your results over time, you can adjust goals to be more meaningful and achievable.

Measuring Tangibles vs. Analyzing Intangibles   Some numbers you want to track are readily available for collection: number of subscribers to your newsletter, books sold, comments posted on your blog. Other trends could be worth paying attention to and analyzing, such as media attention, audience response when you are a guest speaker, and quality of customer referrals.

Course Correction Steps vs. Hit or Miss   Informed decisions almost always beat blind guesses. Although setting up your tracking system takes time up front, it will certainly save time, effort, and money by giving you vital information on your key decision-making indicators. With tracking data in your hand, clarity and confidence will be yours as you make changes in the course of your journey to reach success as you have defined it.

Summary

Because book tracking is critical to discovering how marketing efforts are working in the marketplace, we recommend you set up a tracking matrix on software you already use, update it frequently, and carefully review it at least monthly. Determine what is most useful to measure, but also allow your key indicators to evolve over time. Their purpose is to help you make better decisions and course corrections. Tracking allows you to evaluate trends over time and adjust your marketing accordingly.

Chapter XIII

Get Set To Soar And Sustain Your Success

Cleared for Takeoff

Navigation lights on: *Check.* Taxi lights on: *Check.* Flight plan: *Check.* Flaps set: *Check.* Flight instruments: *Check.* Radios and avionics: *Set for departure.*

Chances are that you may be thinking that "I am an author, not a pilot. What does going through a pre-flight checklist have to do with me and my book?" Our answer is that while there are not mandated procedures as you get ready to declare your book ready to take off and go to market, you can benefit from considering the purpose of a pilot's pre-flight checklist: *final preparation steps matter a great deal and are based on years of experience, sometimes learned the hard way.* In other words, if you have used and applied the chapters in this book as you have been writing, you are almost at your goal of publishing your book. But if you do just a few more things before your book launches with the goal of landing in target readers' hands, the chances of a smooth and successful venture will be enhanced significantly.

Don't Rush To Take Off Into The Publishing World: Get Ahead Of Potential Mistakes With A Thorough Pre-Flight Check

It may be a cliché but it is still true that you only have one chance to make a good first impression. What that means to an author is to be very certain that your book is ready for the world to see before you commit to publishing it. Once you launch your book the whole world *can* see it, almost instantaneously. If there is a mistake in your book or your cover, or in the description and promotional information you have created for your book, and you submit the book for publication, the error will be distributed far and wide. When you start getting emails from readers pointing out the error(s) your soaring sense of accomplishment will crash. From your own web site to heavy-traffic, mega-booksellers like Amazon, the evidence of your misstep will already be out there.

While it is possible to revise and republish your book, that process is time-consuming, costly, and there is no retro-fix for the copies already in your readers' hands. You want to impress target readers with your experience and professionalism, and demonstrate that you have high standards and that you care about your reader. Your editor or publisher has probably encouraged you to keep rolling along and move through the steps to finishing your book, but will not be pushing you to launch, distribute and market your book until you have thoroughly checked your "pre-flight" checklist.

Here are a few things to check before you submit your manuscript and proclaim it to be ready for takeoff into the world of published books.

Editing And Proofreading: The Author's Best Friends

While the terms *proofreading* and *editing* are often used interchangeably, they are different.

Editing is typically completed throughout the writing process – especially between drafts – and often includes changes in context and organization that affect the overall meaning and presentation. The focus is on changes that affect style, point-of-view, organization of content, flow, and choosing the right tone and vocabulary for the particular target readers.

Proofreading occurs later in the writing process, usually just after the final editing and before the final draft that will be presented for publication. The focus is on correcting errors in spelling, syntax, grammar, punctuation, and formatting.

While some editing will inevitably be done during the proofreading process and vice versa—the writing process is not perfectly linear, after all—focusing on proofreading too early in the writing process is often inefficient because with each revision new errors are introduced. Most useful just before launch, proofreading is the process of carefully reviewing a text for errors, especially surface errors such as spelling, punctuation, grammar, formatting, and typing errors.

Proofreading Checklist

□ Punctuation – Periods, commas, hyphens and other marks are in place, with no extra spaces. In a list of bullet points each item either has a period or not (consistency is important.)

□ Word fragments or duplication – Spell-checking will not pick up an error such as 'lean' when the intended word is "learn." Also watch for repeating word errors such as as.

□ Sentence fragments – e.g., "And that was just in the first hundred pages!" On rare occasions, an incomplete sentence can stand. It often begins with "and" but, as with any grammatical rules, rules can occasionally be broken but only with good reason, and on a very occasional basis. By reading in context, you will know if a sentence fragment belongs. Or not.

□ Formatting numbers, special names or titles – For example, in this book, we have created a style manual that uses eBook and eBooks rather than Ebooks or ebooks. We capitalize the "e" in "EBook" only if it is the first word in a sentence, or a capitalized word within a title. We also include a hyphen with E-reader and e-reader. Book titles (and subtitles) are italicized. If in doubt, consult a style manual in widespread use such as the *Associated Press's AP Style Manual.*

□ Paragraph and space formatting – A paragraph should be indented with a tab set of .3 or .5, or whatever you choose as long as it is consistent throughout. There should be one space between sentences, not two. Other formatting errors or inconsistencies should be corrected using your pre-determined plan for items such as fonts and headings.

□ Verb tense and subject/verb agreement are also common but key errors that should be looked for when proofreading. The subject should always agree with the verb in tense and number. These verb issues are often overlooked or unnoticed while writing an initial draft, but can usually be caught with a good proofread. Reading out loud can help get through tricky areas you are proofreading.

Make sure that your manuscript has been thoroughly edited and proofread. You and your editor must carefully organize and reorganize your chapters and sections so that they are easy to read and convey your ideas with accuracy and clarity. Before you commit to publication, take a good look at your table of contents and your outline and make certain that they reflect your intentions as an author. If you have to do some minor additional editing, it is better to do it before publication than to discover things you wish to change after your book has launched.

The Need for Speed: Book Readers Appreciate an Index

Does your nonfiction book need an index? Many do not, but libraries prefer them and so do most reviewers and readers. An index is an alphabetical list of persons, places and subjects mentioned in a book. Usually the index is located among the final pages of a book. The index is the traditional place a reader can look to find a page number (or numbers) where they can find a certain piece of information or key word. In eBooks, the page number is not relevant but the location of the chosen text can be instantly accessed since the indexed words are hyperlinked.

With an eBook, some experts say an index in not necessary because an e-reader has a word search function. The Kindle and other eBook readers offer search technology that allows you to enter a keyword or phrase to find "every instance in your book." The problem is that these search methods are often not user-friendly. With professional indexing, a targeted guide to your book's information is created using main and sub-topics so readers can quickly find exactly what they need. Also there are cross-references between related information, helping readers to recognize the availability of additional information they may not have initially considered.

Creating a proper index is a daunting task and the time needed to create it depends upon your book's length and complexity. However, while you do not *have* to have an index, if your book is on a technical or medical topic, or has many terms and concepts, an index will certainly be appreciated by your readers and enhance your book's likelihood of success.

Formats Are Fickle: Converting For Publication Requires Mastery

We have mentioned this before, but it is so important that it is worth revisiting. Once you are certain that your manuscript is error-free, complete, and ready to publish, the time has come (as outlined in the marketing plan for your book) to format the manuscript into the right files for the right bookstores and distribution channels. As discussed earlier in this book, presently there is no industry standard when you need your manuscript converted into an eBook. Nook e-readers require epub files, for example, while Kindle e-readers require a totally different file structure, and some late models can handle more than one file format, including PDF. The Apple world has still more file requirements, some proprietary and exclusive and some not. Web-based downloads usually are provided in a PDF format, although it is possible to deliver virtually any file format, depending on the author's target market and the distribution formats they expect.

Mastering the current universe of e-readers, browsers, file formats, and steps required to convert your manuscript into the various formats needed requires a steep learning curve. Most authors choose to delegate this job to those who have already put together the puzzle pieces and can quickly handle all the tedious and technical steps of publication. There are resources which provide that service cost-effectively so you can focus on putting your expertise into your book and on getting the word out about it.

Print On Demand (POD) files, too, have their own requirements, so do your homework and prepare them very carefully according to the requirements of the POD service you are using.

Don't Take Off Without A Flight Plan

Once you have your editorial and technical engines checked and up to speed, you are getting much closer to being ready to publish, but you are not quite there yet. You still have a few important pre-flight marketing tasks to finish.

Here is a reminder from what we discussed in Chapter VIII. Since the promotional copy on the back cover of your book is so critical to its marketing success, you should create a back cover description of your book that summarizes its contents and gives reasons to read it that are enticing to your target market. You should also include at least one (and preferably two or three) endorsements by a recognizable authority in the field of your book topic, a raving fan with a high-credibility title or company name, or a famous person with an authentic, even if loose, connection to you and your book. In this example, the author let the testimonial quotes and his own thoughts serve as the book description.

If you want to see many examples of very professional and effective promotional copy, go online to the Amazon bookstore and drill down to Best Sellers, or go to Barnes & Noble online and check out the B&N Top 100 NOOK Book Bestsellers. Look around at the book promotional copy you see there, paying particular attention to books that are similar to your topic. While closely paraphrasing these promotional blurbs is not recommended, and plagiarizing them is illegal, getting an idea for their length and the kind of terms they use will be helpful as you build your own promotional wording, or "copy." You may want your publishing partner to review your promotional copy or write it for you. It is a key factor in book marketing success.

The same promotional copy should be used to describe your book when placed in the various online bookstores along with your front cover graphic. If one of your endorsements is by an instantly recognizable name, you can include a short quote from it.

Here is an example of how a few well-crafted sentences can clinch the decision to buy a book. (Perhaps the book's author had a hand in writing it.)

"Long live the King" hailed *Entertainment Weekly* upon publication of Stephen King's *On Writing*. Part memoir, part master class by one of the bestselling authors of all time, this superb volume is a revealing and practical view of the writer's craft, comprising the basic tools of the trade every writer must have. King's advice is grounded in his vivid memories from childhood through his emergence as a writer, from his struggling early career to his widely reported, near-fatal accident in 1999—and how the inextricable link between writing and living spurred his recovery. Brilliantly structured, friendly and inspiring, *On Writing* will empower and entertain everyone who reads it – fans, writers, and anyone who loves a great story well told."

Once you have the promotional copy ready to go, it's time to review and get ready to use the marketing plan that you developed as you worked with Chapter XI on marketing. Most publishers launch a splashy marketing blitz when they publish a new book. If you are going the self-publishing route without purchasing a marketing plan from your publishing partner, you need to create your plan so you are prepared to launch your own marketing campaign as soon as your book is published. It is the key to soaring vs. falling flat.

Know Your Indicators and Check Your Instruments To Measure Them

If you have done everything in this chapter so far, you're almost ready to publish. There are just two more things that you need to think about and accomplish. Both will measurably increase your chances of long-term success. The first is simple: Review Chapter XII in this book (on tracking) and have your systems in place before you publish. Doing so will insure that you won't miss key variables, and you will have the data in enough time to evaluate short and medium term results and make any necessary changes. A starting flight plan is good, but anticipating course correction is critical.

The second remaining step is a little harder to define than tracking, but it is very important. You need to recognize that publishing your book will affect your personal and business brand. With the surge of social media, you not only have the ability, but you now have the need to manage your own reputation, both online and in real life.

Prospective clients will "google" you before they even initiate an inquiry on your web site or call your office. Many of your current clients and associates are probably following you and your business online as well. You need to have a great, and up-to-date LinkedIn profile because you are building the image of who you are over time, using real and virtual interactions. You want to be in control of all of those impressions, not leave your professional reputation to chance. You want to be the best PR manager of your image and personal brand. Your personal brand is all about who you are and how you want to be known.

Your new book is one of the most powerful ways to enhance your personal brand.

Your book will directly affect how people perceive you. You will instantly become more visible as an expert on the topic of your book, and credited as a "published author." Seriously, the working title for this very book about how to become a published author was, for a time, "Instant Credibility." If you already are a published author, your new book will open the door of opportunity for people to learn about your past publishing accomplishments and your most up-to-date information on your work, your company or your message. The point is, be aware that with the publication of your book, you will be stepping into the spotlight. Just like a final check in the mirror before you go out in public, it is wise to use a checklist before you send your book out to your audience.

Take-Off Is Not The End Goal – It's The Beginning

You may have been so intent on finishing your book and getting the manuscript to this point that you put off fully developing your marketing plan, but now you must put on your marketing strategist's hat. Once you have carefully reviewed all there is to review before publication, you can focus on the action plan to begin as soon as your book appears in the Kindle store and/or other bookselling sites. For example, your brand is a potentially very valuable asset and you should leverage it whenever and wherever possible. Use your "I am a published authority" brand in your email signature. For example:

Joe Adding, CPA
Author of *Saving Money On Next Year's Taxes*
What to do This Year for Big Pay-offs Next Year

When you introduce yourself, even if it is a thirty-second opportunity, remember to include that you recently published a book about your topic. Of course you will also need to update your resume, your social media profiles, bios, and your 'About' information on your web site. Put your book cover graphic in a prominent place on your web site, marketing materials, and even your business card if you wish. Include reference to your book every time you speak to business groups, send a press release, or

223

otherwise market yourself. The point is to keep your new brand top-of-mind, and do what you can to put your brand in front of others so that they will recognize you for what you are: a published author who is on the way to being the go-to person on the topic of your book.

Flying The Friendly Skies: Your Plan For Continued Success

You have come a long way on your journey as an author and are just about ready to publish. But now, right before you take the big step of launching your book, is the best time to plan for future success and evaluate where your book falls into your overall writing and marketing strategy.

Consider, as we pointed out in Chapter XI on marketing, the chances are pretty solid that you have more that is worthwhile to say on the topic. At this point, wouldn't you agree that the process of writing and publishing your *next* book will be easier in most, if not all, respects? Recall all that you learned as you were mind-mapping, researching, outlining, and writing about your topic that was relevant but didn't quite seem to fit into the present book. Once you publish and successfully market your book, people are going to turn to you as the go-to expert on the topic. Don't let them down. Tell them more in another book or a whole series of books. We are confident that you can continue writing, sharing your wisdom with others, for as long as you want, publishing a stack of books to claim as your legacy.

You Are Ready for Take-Off. Push the Throttle NOW.

Mr. or Ms. Author, that moment is here. You have read and made good use of this book, done your pre-publishing homework and written a good book. It's time to publish. We wish you the best. Please let the authors of this book know how you and your book are doing. You can find us at www.suncoastdigitalpress.com.

> "Action is the foundational key to all success."
>
> — Pablo Picasso

Key Distinction For This Chapter

"Good. Enough!" vs. An Infinity Pool It is a bad idea to skip proof-reading or any final wrap-up phases of your book project completion. Note the many important items covered in this chapter. But after those steps are checked off, call it "done," or you could fall into perfectionistic procrastination and work on your book into infinity. (Launch this one and go work on your *next* book!)

Summary

You need to refer to a final checklist so you don't waste the good, hard work you've put in and prematurely launch a book which does not represent all the effort you made to write and produce a great book. You don't want errors and oversights to diminish your chance for success with your book. So, use this chapter to sure everything up…but once you have done so, it is time to launch and guide your book out into the world. Give it the publicity and spotlight it deserves.

Epilogue

Suncoast Digital Press

"The chief glory of every people arises from its authors."
— Samuel Johnson

We, the authors and general editors of this work, have traveled the path you are currently on. We know that this journey is one of life's most satisfying adventures. Digging into your own rich experiences and writing your creative ideas for others to read is a gift you offer to your readers.

Yes, we know that writing and publishing is challenging and requires dedication, but we also know that it is enormously satisfying to write and publish books and join the relatively small group of people who not only want to write a book, but actually do so. As authors of both traditionally published (Harper Collins) books and self-published books and eBooks, we have dealt with the same self-doubts, serious time constraints, and uncertainties about how publishing works. We've also faced the author's uncertainty of success (or fear of failure) because we too have poured out our ideas into our books with no guarantee of being read or appreciated by our readers, or reaping rewards for our labor. And, we have found it is worth every ounce of effort. We think you will too.

You ~~*Should*~~ *Can Write A Book: How to Write What You Know And Self-Publish Your Way to Success* will act as your guide to the self-publishing revolution that has changed, and is continuing to change, the way people write, publish, and market books and eBooks. We also know that to increase your chances of success in today's global-sized bookstores and burgeoning eBook marketplace, it is not enough to "just" write a good book. You also have to publish it in optimal ways that will assist you in marketing it effectively if you are going to take full advantage of the rewards and successes of authorship.

We have presented the steps and explanations needed for a simple book idea to take hold and become a reality, but we do not believe that any individual, no matter how talented and motivated he or she may be, should tackle all these steps alone. Think about what you have learned in this book and which tasks you personally would enjoy and could handle effectively, and which tasks (such as editing, proofreading and marketing) it makes sense to delegate.

Also, it is important to keep in mind that professional skills and good tools are imperative for writers. As you use them, play to your own strengths and remember we are here to help you find and use resources you need at any step along the way.

"Always bear in mind that your own resolution to succeed is more important than any other."

— Abraham Lincoln

Acknowledgements

The development and publication of this book is the result of our combined experience of more than a century in pursuit of word mastery. From our early family upbringings which taught the value and importance of reading, to the many dedicated and competent teachers and inspirational writers, there are literally thousands of people to acknowledge. If you, our dear reader, have ever taught or encouraged others to read, write, and love books and the pursuit of knowledge, we also want to acknowledge you, because you are exactly who is behind the creation of this book.

In particular, we would like to thank and acknowledge those who were there for the beginning, muddle, and end of this book project. (That wasn't a typo.) Without your support and contributions, this book would not be. So thank you, with deepest appreciation, Ginny Orenstein, Roni Belmont, Eric Belmont, Fred Bingham, Avarie Hannah, Ted Radford, George Schofield, Teresa Bueno, Nick Gladding, Jill Green and Ed Bernica.

Barbara Bingham and Jeff Orenstein

Contact The Authors

The authors and general editors want to be your continuing publishing resource long after you have read and used this book.

- Please keep in touch with us by visiting our website at

www.SuncoastDigitalPress.com

We recommend that you bookmark it and return there from time to time because it changes often. There you will find free reports, an offer for a free author assessment, videos, and many other features and ideas of interest to authors.

- While you are on our site, please be sure to read our blog, including back issues. We use the blog as a forum for author guidance, observations, and publishing news of relevance to authors.

- Please add your name to our mailing list because we publish a free newsletter once in a while and we can notify you of webinars (many without cost) that will help you.

- We also invite you to like our Facebook page at http://www.Facebook.com/DynamicEBooks and to join in the dialogue there. We will continue to use it to publish more free tips on eBook/book authoring and marketing.

- We post occasional things of interest to authors on Twitter at /twitter.com/Jeffpublisher and urge you to follow us, and you can also view many author-related videos on the Suncoast Digital Press YouTube channel, including the videos in this eBook.

Keep Up Or Be Left Behind

The eBook revolution is in its infancy. The future of eBooks is bright, dynamic and exciting. We are certain that eBooks will become the dominant book mode within a few years, and we are equally certain that technology will continue to evolve. In the fast-moving field of digital publishing, just as in life, the only constant is change. For that reason, we urge you to keep up with changes in the field as you plan, write and publish your books. We have included the current state-of-the-art eBook technology and industry information in this book as of this writing. As changes come, we will write about them in our blogs and in subsequent editions of this book as needed.

Best Wishes For Your Self-Publishing Success!

Thank you for reading (and using!) this book and please accept our best wishes for your continuing success as an author. We are looking forward to hearing from you and to reading your books. Welcome to the self-publishing revolution!

"Books are the compasses and telescopes and sextants and charts which other men have prepared to help us navigate the dangerous seas of human life."

– Jesse Lee Bennett

Barbara Bingham

Jeffrey R. Orenstein, Ph.D,

About The Authors

Barbara Bingham, President, Suncoast Digital Press, Inc.

Barbara Bingham self-published her first book at age seven, handling not only the story-writing but the crayon illustrations, cover design, and stapling. Technology has thankfully come a long way since then, and she currently has three books selling on Amazon and in other major book stores.

While a dedicated writer and magazine columnist, Barbara is most passionate about working with others – encouraging, teaching, and coaching them to write, finish and publish the book(s) they've always dreamed of writing. Coaching is natural for Bingham as she has extensive training and experience as a professional coach to small business owners, professionals in private practice, and adults with AD/HD. She is a graduate and former faculty member of Coach U, and achieved the highest credential in the field of professional coaching, the International Coaching Federation (ICF) *Master Certified Coach.*

Bingham helps people from all backgrounds become published authors. Though her clients include a 90-year-old gentleman publishing his first book of poetry, her specialty is nonfiction business and self-help books whose primary purpose is to catapult the author's reputation, personal brand, and credibility.

As a lifelong entrepreneur, Bingham knows the importance of strategic marketing which helps one stand out, exude excellence, and attract ideal clients. She believes that writing a book does this better and faster than any other means within the professional's control. As founder and former CEO of Planet Computer Services, Inc. (Atlanta, GA,) Bingham learned the value of leveraging your expertise as the most affordable way to advertise and reach your target market. In her ten years as a professional coach in private practice (Charleston, SC,) Bingham found that no matter what your business or personal goals are, being a published author can, and did, help many of her clients succeed in building their reputation and revenues.

A native Floridian, Bingham is a graduate of Florida State University, and of graduate studies at the American College of Switzerland.

Co-founder and president of Suncoast Digital Press, Inc. (Sarasota, FL,) Bingham currently acts as a publishing partner, editor, and coach to those with the desire and commitment to write a nonfiction book. *You ~~Should~~ Can Write A Book: How To Write What You Know And Self-Publish Your Way To Success* is the culmination of her own hands-on experience and expertise in independent publishing. She preaches what she practices, presenting teleclasses and webinars and speaking to groups and organizations about the self-publishing revolution. She serves as President of Toastmasters International's south Sarasota club, and volunteers as a mentor and fundraiser for *The Y-Foundation's* children's programs. For more information about her publishing company, or for additional self-publishing resources including free special reports authored by Bingham, please visit www.SuncoastDigitalPress.com.

Jeffrey R. Orenstein, Ph.D, Editor and Publisher

Suncoast Digital Press is the latest chapter in a life in writing and publishing for Jeffrey R. Orenstein, Ph.D.. At the age of 11, he started his own neighborhood newspaper in Cleveland, where he was born. As an undergrad at Ohio State, his first professional byline was for the university newspaper. During his career as a political science professor, he wrote several textbooks and public policy analyses for Harper Collins, Praeger, Kendall Hunt and others, and scores of policy monographs for professional meetings. He was also a manuscript evaluation reader for several major publishers.

Upon retiring as a full professor, he took up freelance business writing and journalism and published articles in national magazines (including one published by IBM) and newspapers.

In Florida, where he has lived since 1995, he was a columnist for the *Boca Raton Business Journal*, and then became Executive Editor of the *Gulf Coast Business Review* and created and became the first Executive Editor of the community newspaper for Lakewood Ranch, Florida. He also started and currently co-publishes and writes for *Living On The Suncoast*, a greater Sarasota glossy lifestyle magazine.

He was one of the founders of Suncoast Digital Press, Inc., and continues to serve that company's clients as an editorial and eBook consultant. He is the author of *Words @ Work*, an eBook on business writing, and this volume, both published by Suncoast Digital Press, Inc.

Orenstein has a B.A. from Ohio State University and an M.A. and Ph.D from the University of Wisconsin-Madison, all in political science. He was a political science professor at a large Midwestern university for 25 years and retired as a full professor.

In his leisure time, he follows politics and public policy, is an avid photographer, reader, train buff, model railroader, jazz fan, wine collector and community volunteer. He serves on the board of directors of the Manatee Chamber of Commerce and the Manatee Rural Health Foundation. He also is a county-appointed representative to the Community Advisory Boards of the Sarasota-Manatee Metropolitan Planning Organization, and the Tampa Bay Regional Transportation Authority.

We hope you've enjoyed this book, and that you have already started to put it to good use – it is only as good as the books it inspires! Please visit our web site for information on our new webinars, workshops and teleclasses based on this book.

Thank you!

Barbara Bingham & Jeff Orenstein

www.SuncoastDigitalPress.com

www.ingramcontent.com/pod-product-compliance
Lightning Source LLC
Chambersburg PA
CBHW060305100426

42742CB00011B/1867